CURIOPTICALS

Dedication:

I dedicate this optical illusion book to a small village and its inhabitants, where I spent my childhood surrounded by dreams and illusions. The mysterious Norman castle of Quaglietta (*Aquae Electae*, in Latin), destroyed by an earthquake in 1980, will always enchant my memories.

GIANNI A. SARCONE

THIS IS A CARLTON BOOK

Artworks and Text © 2009 Archimedes' Laboratory Limited
Design © 2009 Carlton Books Limited

This edition published 2009 by
Carlton Books Limited
20 Mortimer Street
London W1T 3JW

ISBN 978-1-84732-229-6

Printed and bound in China

Picture Credits:
Scott Blake, page 54;
István Orosz, pages 66 and 68;
Rusty Rust, pages 117 and 123.

CURIOPTICALS

Being an historical examination and portrayal,
a journey through more than 150 years of
the art of the craftsman of deceitful imagery,
devised for the specific purposes of misleading,
hoodwinking, suckering and generally confusing
the human brain, eyes and associated organs,
and written, researched and collated by the
esteemed gentleman Mr Gianni A. Sarcone

CARLTON
BOOKS

INTRODUCTION

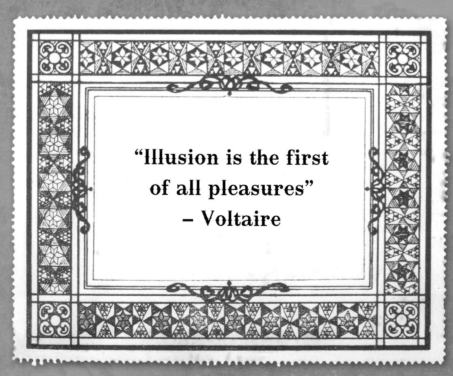

"Illusion is the first
of all pleasures"
– Voltaire

A Ticket to visual amazement!

Ladies and gentlemen, get your Curiopticals tickets and get ready for the greatest show on earth! The illusionary big top is coming to town, along with fun and wonder for ladies and gentlemen of all ages... Optical illusions have been a source of joy and wonder since the earliest days of humanity. They're still as compelling today, a guaranteed source of thrills, amazement and laughter.

One of the main attractions of any optical illusion show – Curiopticals included, of course – is the incredible array of classic optical illusions. Some are famous, whilst others are lesser known and revisited, but they are all breathtaking. Starting from the earliest experimental images, Curiopticals features all kinds of fascinating optical illusions from throughout history and across all the continents... Distortions of perception, size and shape confusion, ambiguous and topsy-turvy figures, hidden shapes, and magical impossible objects are all stock in trade for the classic and vintage optical illusions. Curiopticals also offers a range of more exotic optical illusions, such as incredible colour effects, illusory self-moving patterns, interactive optical conjuring and mind reading tricks, and last – but not least – a baffling visual levitation!

But there's more to all of this than just the sheer joy of illusion, however. Curiopticals includes a stack of fascinating information that will help shed light on how the scientific principles that underlie many illusions work, and reveal some of the long and captivating history of illusion-making. There's a whole range of amazing ancient optical devices to wow you, such as the thaumatrope, the daguerreotype (with a picture of the first man ever photographed!), and the stereoscope... It is amusing and revealing to realise that our grandfathers were as fond of visual teasing as we ourselves are.

Curiopticals gives you the chance to not only admire, but also to take part and measure your knowledge of optical illusions by answering intriguing questions. These include "To your mind, are these optical illusion cards from 1760, 1880 or from 1920?" "Could you tell the real ancient images from the modern imitations?" "Who was the mysterious artist and who was the detractor?" In fact, Curiopticals will also unmask some scientists and artists who posed themselves as authors of well-known optical illusions.

Curiopticals is your chance to enjoy the amazing optical illusions and visual curiosities that have survived across the world's cultures down through the centuries. Be there for the spectacular opening, and stay till the Grand Finale. You won't be disappointed!

Your showman,
Gianni A. Sarcone
The Master of Deception
Designer and co-founder of Archimedes-lab.org

About the Authors of the Book

Gianni A. Sarcone and Marie-Jo Waeber, the founders and the editors of the Archimedes' Lab website, are freelance writers, popularizers and illustrators. Experts in mind games and brain training, they are particularly involved in cognitive sciences (teaching methodology, creativity and communication) and have written numerous books on topics ranging from optical illusions to visual and critical thinking puzzles. Sarcone is also a leading authority on visual perception – he was one of the judges at the third "Best Visual Illusion of the Year Contest" held in Sarasota, Florida, USA. Sarcone and Waeber are also contributing editors to the successful popular science magazines *Focus BrainTrainer*, *Focus Junior*, and *Focus Extra* (Italy). You can get more info about their activities at: http://www.archimedes-lab.org/fornewspapers.

The Fertile Eyes of the Mind

Our brain is an artist that paints the reality that surrounds us. It transforms energy into colour; links distances, movement and form to create reality in 3D; interprets visual stimuli and compares them to memories... and sometimes, it makes mistakes.

Are the eyes an open door to the world, as poets say? Well, honestly, not really. The fact is, we see the world through a pair of tiny peepholes, the pupils of our eyes. Our brain functions as a highly creative 'camera obscura' – the forerunner of the modern photographic camera, named from the Latin for dark room. The brain elaborates the visual stimuli we receive, transforming them into true artworks. The German poet Novalis said that the eye is a 'superficial' organ. That is indeed partly true. We will even add that it is an external organ: the eye with which we see the world is a part of the world itself. As soon as we open the eye, whup, the world pops in it!

The eye is a humble and silent organ. It cannot 'see' itself, and is itself unnoticed in use. Moreover, unlike a camera, the eye 'creates' a field of vision without real edges. That seems paradoxical at first glance, that our field of vision is limited but does not have boundaries... There are no blank zones outside of our visual field. Our brain simply cancels out those edges with a smooth fade-out effect.

In English, there are two essential families of words that we use to express the faculty and the act of seeing: 1) 'sight', 'see', and 2) 'vision', 'view'. Looking at these words etymologically, it seems most probable that they originally came from words that meant, respectively, "to follow something with the eyes" (from the Indo-European *seqw-) and "to have learned" (from the Indo-European *weid-). This suggests that, for our ancestors, an image was something to shape with the eyes (follow with the eye), a form of information taken from the real world (learning through visual perception).

Vision, though, doesn't actually correspond to the direct perception of reality, and neither is it an innate process. It depends to a large extent on ability acquired through a long and laborious undertaking. We take the concept of vision for granted, but a person who is blind from birth, who later in life gains the sense of sight, takes many years to learn how to understand and organize the things that he now perceives. The ability to see is a process far from banal, and far from being passive. When we look at a panorama, its colours take around 30 milliseconds to arrive at the 'visual cortex' within the posterior lobes of our brain (also known as 'striate cortex' or 'V1'). The shapes of the scene, and the sensation of the distances – which involve depth and motion – are perceived shortly after, at approximately 70 milliseconds. During these tiny slices of time, the brain filters, analyses, and interprets the various pieces of the perceptive puzzle, trying to assemble them into a coherent image. In other words, it is crafting the best and most useful scene possible from the raw image data that our eyes present to us. Without the active involvement of the brain (and taking into consideration only a few major visual issues), we would probably see the world as monochromatic, upside down and with a very large hole in the middle. This last section corresponds to the very real 'blind spot' we all have where the optical nerve enters the eye.

The important thing for us of course is that because it does so much hard work when we look at things, the brain can be tricked. In this book, we will specifically focus on ancient and vintage optical illusions and visual 'mirabilia' throughout the ages. You will, of course, also find recreations of ancient illusions, and lesser-known new illusions. You can challenge yourself by guessing which are real ancient illusions and which are new ones! In short, this book is an examination of the historical aspects of visual illusion and optical curiosity. You'll find a greater supply of modern visual tricks in our previous books *New Optical Illusions*, *Fantastic Optical Illusions*, *What Are You Looking At?*, *Puzzillusions* and *Eye Tricks*, along with comprehensive information concerning the scientific and psychological aspects of the visual illusion.

How we see

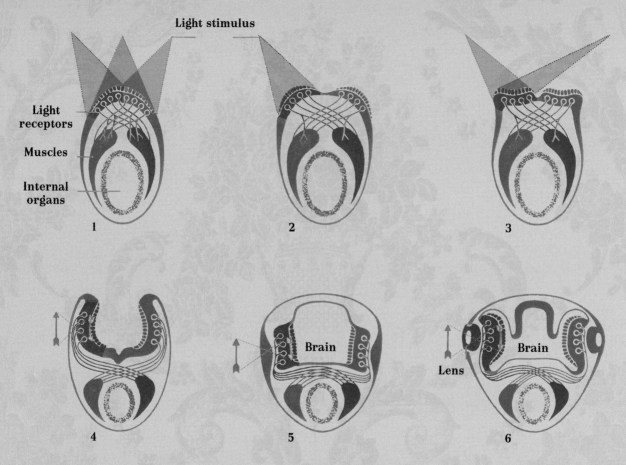

(Drawing adapted after the 'The Vertebrate Visual System' by Otto van Eersel, 1955)

"No man has ever seen the Light; but we see by reason of it
those objects which reflect the light"
– Eliphas Levi

The birth of vision

The first animals with anything resembling an eye lived about 550 million years ago. According to scientist Stephen Polyak, those ancestral creatures had a simple light-sensitive patch on the skin that gave them some tiny survival advantage (see fig. 1 of the image 'Eye Evolution'). This perhaps allowed them to turn towards light, or to evade a predator that cast a shadow. Evolutionary changes then separated the light-sensitive patch of the micro-organism into two eyespots (see fig. 2 and 3) – the different positions of the eyes on the head could have helped a creature to more accurately distinguish the orientation of the light, and would eventually allow depth perception. Progressively, over millennia, a deepening pit was created, and the light-sensitive patches of cells (the future retinas) turned to face each other (fig. 4). Simplified images were then able to form on both patches thanks to the skin becoming translucent. At the same time, the pits openings gradually narrowed, until the eyes became separated by the brain (fig. 5). Finally, crystalline lenses formed so that, like a pinhole camera, light entered through two small apertures, making 'vision' sharper. Vertebrates and octopuses developed the camera eye independently – our version is less efficient, because the nerve fibres pass in front of the retina.

Scientists calculated that 'only' 364,000 years would have been needed for a quick-breeding species to evolve a camera-like eye from a light-sensitive patch. Nowadays, the smallest primitive creature on earth able to see images is the Copilia Quadrata, a 2mm-long micro-organism (tail included!) of the family of crustaceans which has two lateral eyes, each of which possesses a pair of lenses.

However, only a few animals can see colours, including man and the other primates, fish, amphibians, and some birds. But most of these animals have a relatively primitive form of colour vision, limited to blue and yellow light. Only a small group of primates have full colour vision ranging from red to green as well as blue-yellow. Scientists believe that the ability to see in colour – and specifically to distinguish red from green – emerged because it helped our ancestors to forage for food. It could have been important to them to help better distinguish ripe red fruits from green leaves. Fruits of course contain higher proteins and are easier to digest, so fruit-eating ancestors of ours would have been less likely to starve. As we can see however, the process of the evolution of colour vision still continues!

"What is a television apparatus to man, who has only to shut his eyes to see the most inaccessible regions of the seen and the never seen, who has only to imagine in order to pierce through walls and cause all the planetary Baghdads of his dreams to rise from the dust"
– Salvador Dalí

A biophysical phenomenon

The Greek philosopher Empedocles (490–430 B.C.) suggested that 'effluences' emanated by bodies enter the eye, and then some element in the eye distinguished light from dark to form visual images. Plato proposed another theory about our visual perception that has very little in common with our modern explanations – he thought that sight was not based on light rays entering the eye, but on 'rays of vision' extending from the eye that then interacted with particles emanating from bodies. So, a lot of confusing theories competed for a long period of time and we had to wait until the 17th century to really understand the basic mechanisms of vision.

Vision begins with light. The Bible narrates that God commanded "let there be light" on the first day of Creation, demonstrating the importance of light in the beginning process of life. Man has known since antiquity that light can be separated with a prism into a band of colours – as seen in a rainbow – but it wasn't until the 17th century that scientists discovered the principle that underlies it. Colour is in fact energy, an electromagnetic phenomenon which depends on the way that light is reflected by objects. Every object absorbs a certain part (a selection of wavelengths) of the light which hits it, and deflects the rest. This reflected light is interpreted by our brain as having a particular colour. We shouldn't, therefore, be surprised to find that the word colour comes from the Latin root celare, 'that which covers or conceals'. Colour is already an illusion per se, a ghost that takes life only in our visual system when light stimulates the photo-receptors – the antennae that pick up luminous signals – that fill in the background of our eyes. In reality, the world surrounding us is monochrome.

But there is also another trick. Although the eye measures colour partly on the basis of the frequency of light that hits it, it also judges every colour in relation to other colours nearby. A colour is perceived to be brighter, for example, if it is surrounded by a complementary colour – two colours are said to be complementary if together their radiation produces white. It is also seen as lighter if the background colour is darker. Then there is a mechanism that enhances the contrast of the outline of an object relative to its background. This is called 'lateral inhibition', because each group of photo-receptors – creating a small receptive field – tends to inhibit the response of the other one that surrounds it. The result is that things which appear to be clearly defined become even more so, and vice versa. The same mechanism works for colours, too. When photo-receptors from one area of the retina become stimulated by a colour, those next to it become less sensitive to that colour. So, for example, the light blue of a small square that you see on a blue background appears clearer to us than it would do on a yellow background, because yellow contains no blue. An everyday example is given when we watch television. We can see all the hues and luminous intensities of the program, black included, but the black we perceive is actually the original grey colour of the TV screen. It only appears black because of its interaction with other colours nearby!

A mental and philosophical aspect

As many people have said, a picture paints a thousand words. The persuasive power of images is so strong that they can lead you astray, and can easily be used as instruments of propaganda.

Actually, the greatest optical illusion of all is to believe that an image has only one interpretation!

There is little or no questioning of the conventional uses of images, and often photographs are treated as transparent windows on what they are meant to represent – which carries the risk of producing an opposite meaning! Here is an illuminating example: we can use the same shot representing a flock of sheep grazing in front of a nuclear power station to support either an anti-nuclear or a pro-nuclear campaign, because it can be interpreted differently depending on the context as well as on the viewer's inclination. In fact, for nuclear promoters the message is: "animals are grazing peacefully just near a nuclear power station, so nuclear power is not as dangerous as some would suggest." On the other hand, anti-nuclear campaigners would see the message as: "nuclear power is encroaching even on our farming land and contaminating our food supply."

We are even mocked by our self image... When you look in the mirror, do you see what you really look like? Actually, even though you are used to the image, that familiar person isn't really you, it is a flipped version, with the heart on the right and the liver on the left. This might explain why many of us don't like our portrait photos: the image we have of ourselves is always inverted.

Our visual system is a wonderfully sophisticated mechanism for imaging the visible world, but is also a biased instrument and a mediocre, pitiless judge. Our vision system is iconic. We tend to mentally simplify an image in order to better memorise it. Some images are so crystalized in our mind that they become icons, important and enduring symbols. But reality and 'iconic representation' are two very different things. The famous photo of Albert Einstein sticking out his tongue represents just one very minor aspect of the famous mathematician. The Beatles and Marylin Monroe are relevant iconic freeze-frames of our memory. Today,

the Beatles might not have had the same success they had in the 60s, because the visual support provided by a compact disk is very different to that of a vinyl record.

If light is so important to our sight, why then do we spend about one-tenth of our day physiologically blind? Have you ever asked yourself how our sense of sight collaborates and integrates with the other sense organs? What is going on when we see, walk, speak, feel and touch all at the same time?

"For the great majority of mankind are satisfied with appearances, as though they were realities, and are often more influenced by the things that seem than by those that are"
– Niccolò Machiavelli

What links our sight with the sense of touch or hearing? Our sense of vision is tidily connected in to all the other sense organs. We can, to a certain extent, 'see' with hearing, with touch, or even with smell! Just think, for instance, how a smell can evoke or reinforce the image of a fruit. At the same time, eyesight can deceive the other sense organs. For example, when you are in a train at a station, looking out of the window at another neighbouring train that starts moving, you can get the strong sensation that your own train is actually moving in the opposite direction.

We are like sponges absorbing changes in the physical world around us. Our sense organs continuously check for changes in our immediate environment, to allow us to act and react accordingly. But actually we perceive only one percent of what we see in focus at any one time! That's because sensing is not perceiving. Sensing is the passive transmission of information from the outside world to the brain. It is labelled passive because we do not have to be consciously engaging in a 'sensing' process. Perception, on the other hand, is the active process of selecting, organising, and interpreting the information or stimuli brought to the brain by the senses. Thus, we can unconsciously sense a visual stimulus – such as a light beam – but we perceive it only when our brain interprets it (a face? a landscape?) Vision is therefore a mental process, an embryonic form of thinking.

When we observe a scene, we are convinced that we see a complete image. In reality however, we focus only upon some aspects or details of the scene. The rest is created by our memory, experience and/or imagination. Therefore, the impression that we can perceive everything at once, have a 'big picture' of a scene, is just a mere illusion. The reality is that we actually see very little - only that which we are concentrating on or which we find important. Without the crutches of the other sense organs, we would be truly lost, because it is these which permit us, subconsciously, to go about our everyday lives. A famous experiment demonstrated how at times we can be genuinely blind in the truest sense of the word. In this experiment on 'inattentional blindness', carried out in 1999, Daniel Simons and Christopher Chabris asked volunteers to watch a video clip of a basketball game and count the number of times one of the two teams took possession of the ball. As many as 40% of the volunteers failed to see a man dressed up as a gorilla entering from the right, doing a jig in the centre of the screen, and then leaving stage left. The experiment clearly demonstrated that we just don't see what we're not paying attention to, even when it's something totally new and unexpected right in front of our eyes! It's an impressive confirmation of the old saying that "the best place to hide anything is in plain view."

Our experience of the world is forever equivocal. The sheen of a pearl, our partner's voice, the silky smooth touch of a rose, the scent of an apple, all the things that we perceive and feel are just shadows of reality, an infinite train of nerve impulses woven by the brain into a mesmerising net. If these nerve impulses are not truly a reflection of reality then, how do we know anything for sure? In fact, unluckily, the only things that we cannot doubt are our emotions. One cannot doubt that one is happy, sad, in love, or in grief, when such states apply. The only other thing we cannot doubt is... to doubt! The philosopher Descartes based his philosophy upon the 'certainty of doubt' – when all else fails, you cannot actually doubt that you are having doubts.

Given all that, should we disbelieve what we see? No, of course not. Eyesight is very reliable and important for everyday life. We just wanted to make you aware of some of the sensory paradoxes that can occur in particular areas of our life. Don't be as sceptical as the man in the following short story...

A young man found himself sharing a train with his maths professor, a man well known for being a determined empiricist (empiricism is the theory that all true knowledge has to be derived from direct sensory experience). Desperate to strike up a conversation, the young man scanned the horizon hoping for something to remark on. He spotted a field of sheep, and said "Ah, it looks like those sheep have just been sheared," hoping to impress his professor with his powers of observation. The professor regarded the pastoral scene for a moment, and then nodded his head and remarked, "You're right... on the side facing us, anyway."

A Very Short History of Vision and Optical Illusions

If visual illusions have existed since the dawn of time, what is the oldest human optical illusion? Perhaps it was performed by the first prehistoric woman to put on make-up... Joking aside, it can easily be deduced that the concept of optical illusion is as old as man himself. Notwithstanding the lack of any written evidence, the first human beings would certainly have noticed optical phenomena such as mirages, the size of the Moon at its zenith, sticks or poles which appear to be broken in two when half-immersed in water, an after-image from glancing at the sun... There is no doubt, in fact, that our ancestors were aware that optical illusions sometimes occur! Even if they didn't always recognize the physical or cerebral mechanisms that created them, they wondered to themselves, "was it my brain or my eyes that were playing tricks on me?"

From the times of the earliest civilizations right up to the present day, artists, philosophers, and scientists have attempted to give explanations and meanings to the perceivable world that surrounds us and the way we interact with it. Optical illusions have played a constructive role in this search for 'truth' – it has been extremely useful to know how we can be fooled, giving us ever-better understanding of the functioning of our brains. By discovering our weaknesses and limitations, we also created tools to extend our senses in ways which help us discover the elements of the world that are not immediately apparent.

"The eyes and ears are bad witnesses when they are at the service of minds that do not understand their language," said the philosopher Parmenides of Elea 25 centuries ago. A later Greek philosopher, Epicharmus of Kos, believed that our senses were not paying enough attention, and were messing up. He explained, "The mind sees and the mind hears. The rest is blind and deaf." Protagoras, a contemporary of Epicharmus, disagreed. He thought that our senses and body were just fine, and believed that it was the environment that was messing us up. He maintained that man is nothing but a bundle of sensations. One hundred years later, the philosopher Aristotle agreed with both of the rivals, concluding both Epicharmus and Protagoras were jointly right and wrong. He said our senses can

be trusted, but they can be easily fooled. Finally, one of the greatest Greek philosophers, Plato, confirmed around 300 BC that our five senses need our mind to help interpret what they see. In his words, "we must perceive objects through the senses but with the mind," so that the eyes and mind need to work together in the process of vision. That is exactly what scientists still maintain today.

Since the middle of the 19th century, optical illusions have interested scientists and have been used as scientific tests to assess our visual perception. In 1826, Johannes P. Müller, –a German ichthyologist, a scientist who specialised in studying fish! – wrote two books about visual illusions: *Zur vergleichenden Physiologie des Gesichtssinns* (*Regarding the Comparative Physiology of Visual Illusion*) and *Über die phantastischen Gesichtserscheinungen* (*All About Fantastic Visual Illusions*). Unfortunately, almost no-one knew what he was talking about, because he was the first person to refer to 'distortions' as visual illusions. A few years later, in 1851, Adolf Eugen Fick, a German physiologist, described some geometric illusions in his doctoral thesis: *De errore quodam optico asymmetria bulbi effecto* (*The Errors Resulting from Optical Asymmetry*). Shortly afterwards, in 1854, the psychologist J. J. Oppel continued where Müller had left off, by publishing a ten-page article about line illusions – a line appears longer when divided into segments than it does when only its end segments are present. Short as it was, his modest contribution is regarded as the first scientific analysis of optical illusions. In 1860, the German astrophysicist Johann Karl Zöllner became the first to notice that lines which were parallel appeared diagonal in a particular pattern designed as a dress fabric print, and wrote an article on this optical illusion. In 1889, another German psychiatrist, Franz Müller-Lyer, introduced what is now called the Müller-Lyer illusion – one of the most famous, in which identical parallel lines with arrow-like ends appear different lengths depending on whether the ends are pointing inwards or outwards. Twelve theories were created to explain the illusion.

Other remarkable scientists and researchers brought a wide range of very significant contributions to the understanding of the visual perception. Some of the more important include Louis Albert Necker ("Necker cube", 1832), Johann Christian Poggendorff (1860), Ewald Hering (1861), Wilhelm Wundt (1865), Ernst Mach ("Mach bands"), Joseph Jastrow (1889), Wilhelm von Bezold, James Fraser ("Fraser spiral", 1908), Mario Ponzo (1913), Edgar Rubin ("Rubin's vase", 1915), Friedrich Sander ("Sander's parallelogram", 1926), A. Galli ("Galli's triangle", 1931), Adelbert Ames ("Ames' room", 1934), William Orbison (1939), Walter Ehrenstein (1941), and Gaetano Kanizsa ("Kanizsa triangle", 1955). Some of the above illusions are reproduced or described in the following pages.

Scientific publication on the subject of visual illusion increased as public interest developed in the subject. During this period, a lot of optical novelties, games and devices were invented and distributed. The interest in optical illusions is still strong today – we have tons of books and web pages about them. They entertain us, and they can be so useful (or disastrous!) that they have been, and still are, utilised (or counteracted) by skilled artists and artisans. Architects, visual artists, designers, and decorators all regularly use them to aesthetically correct or enhance the appearance of their creations. Real things can often appear deceptive and 'discordant'... The idea of course is to produce a pleasant sensory quality in the object, painting or building. Sometimes the goal is to impress, confuse, or trick the spectator/observer by creating objects in space that seem larger or smaller than they really are. Stage artists employ these tricks to carry the audience's imagination to other suggestive environments or to far countries. Conjurors have utilised them in their shows. Hunters and soldiers use them to advantage creating deceptions to lure prey or fool enemies.

Most optical illusions were first discovered by people who produced textures and patterns whilst working within a wide range of the creative arts, long before being rediscovered and 'officially' described by scientists. Optical illusions were used regularly by artists from Hellenic times through to the medieval period for aesthetic purposes – to create the illusion of spatial harmony, or to give the spectator a feeling of depth, perspective and volume. In fact, a sort of miracle occurs when you view a skilled artwork: the flat image is transformed into a three-dimensional scene in your mind without conscious effort! This is in part due to a drawing technique called 'linear perspective'. Amazingly, the trick of drawing in linear perspective was only invented in the early 15th century by the Genovese architect Leone Battista Alberti, drawing on the groundbreaking work of a contemporary Florentine artisan-engineer, Filippo Brunelleschi. Brunelleschi demonstrated the first trick of perspective with an experiment involving a mirror and a painted panel with a hole, known as 'Brunelleschi's peepshow'. This established forever the validity of projection as a method to create the illusion of depth. Alberti then refined the ideas, creating true linear perspective. In a perspective drawing, every collection of parallel lines in the three-dimensional scene converges to a point in the drawing, called the 'vanishing point', whilst the 'horizon line' defines the eye level. Between the two, a three-dimensional scene appears to be created.

Brunelleschi's peepshow brings us neatly to another important early device in the world of vision – the camera obscura. A camera obscura is simply a darkened room in which the real image of an object is projected through a small opening or lens – the pinhole – and focused in natural colour onto a facing surface. This is unlike a modern camera, because the image is temporary, projected rather than recorded on a film or plate. See the image on page 16 for a portable camera obscura reproduced from "A Treatise on Optics" by Sir David Brewster.

Although the principles of the pinhole camera have been known since antiquity, the camera obscura was first described by Ibn al-Haitham in his *Kitab al-manazir* (*Book of Optics*, 10th century). Its potential as a drawing aid may have been familiar to artists by as early as the 15th century. In fact, Leonardo da Vinci (1452–1519) described the camera obscura principle in his Codex Atlanticus. The Dutch Master painters of the Dutch Golden Age (17th Century), such as Johannes Vermeer, were known for their magnificent attention to detail. It has been widely speculated that they made use of camera obscuras as compositional aids. While the controversy regarding Vermeer's composition may not have been resolved, most scholars agree that many early 'modern' artists were interested in optical devices, and may have been inspired by the visual effects produced by such instruments. Of course, the camera obscura was also an important mean for theorizing about the nature of vision in the early modern period, and it represents a break with the old way of perceiving and representing the world. It is also a good place to end our travels through the world of vision.

So why do most people like optical illusions? Perhaps it is because illusions appear magical. As Rod Serling wrote, "In any quest for magic, in any search for sorcery, witchery, legerdemain, first check the human heart." Each one of us has his own reasons for appreciating the surprise or puzzlement of visual illusions. Some, with a scientific instinct, love searching for the reasons and logical explanations behind them (thinking they are smart enough to figure it out!) Others, perhaps with a more artistic background, are attracted by the aesthetics. More still may be tantalised by the philosophical or contemplative aspect of the illusions, or might be inspired by the seeming glimpses of wonder and impossibility.

The craze for visual illusions must also be considered in light of mankind's thirst of knowledge, of course. Since the Industrial Revolution – coinciding with the Victorian Era – the interest in technologies and disciplines that shed light on our mental processes and behaviour has grown exponentially. The general public seems even more inquisitive now than in the past! What motivates this curiosity? The 'occult' world of the mind, its nature, its mechanism and paradoxes... these things are fascinating to modern mankind, because the consciousness of how the mind works helps us to have a better awareness of ourselves.

Detractors suggest that people who like to be fooled by optical illusions are 'big kids'. We would rather suggest that the marvel of an optical illusion simply takes us back to the spirit of our childhood, a nostalgia that haunts every one of us.

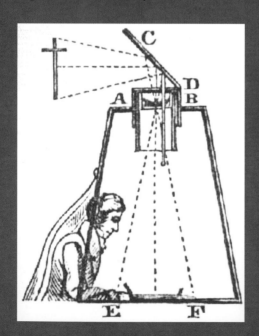

Types of Optical Illusions

What is an illusion? Vision depends, obviously, on the eyes to see – on the photo-receptors we call rods and cones – and on the brain to make sense of what we see. Sometimes the brain is deceived by information received from the eyes. Optical illusions are caused when differences occur between our perceptions or expectations and the image seen by the eye. In fact, there are particular illusions which deceive the human visual system into perceiving something that is not present, or failing to perceive what is present.

Optical illusions can be roughly categorised into four groups. These are:
- physical illusions,
- physiological illusions,
- cognitive illusions, and
- psychopathological illusions.

Physical illusions are phenomenological illusions which occur before light enters the eye - such as a mirage, or a rainbow. Physiological illusions are due to the mechanical structure itself of the eye, and are caused by prolonged stimulation of a specific type (such as brightness, tilt, colour and movement). Cognitive illusions occur in the mind, where the eye's signals interact with our perceptual processing and inbuilt assumptions in such a way that our 'knowledge' becomes misdirected. When we experience a cognitive visual illusion, the error remains compelling even when we are fully aware of its nature. These kinds of illusions are, hence, exceedingly difficult to overcome! Cognitive illusions are commonly sub-divided into ambiguous illusions, distorting illusions and paradoxical illusions. Finally, psychopathological illusions are defined as the morbid perception of objects that are genuinely not there to all but a single observer. These are more commonly known as hallucinations, and may occur in an altered mind-state. This book, obviously, is concerned with the middle two categories of illusion.

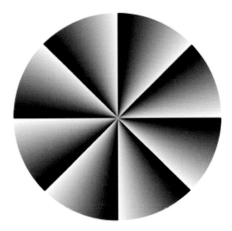

While fixating here, the discs will counterotate!

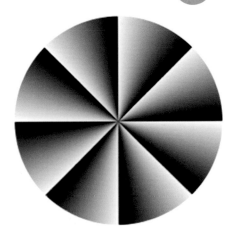

Early Artistic Optical Illusions

The vintage optical illusions in this book fall mostly within four main types:
– hidden figures,
– multipart and composite figures,
– illusive 'vanitas',
– ambiguous and reversible figures.

Hidden figures

When an artist notices that two different things can have a similar appearance, and draws or paints a picture making this similarity evident, he creates what we call an image with double meaning. Many of these images tend to be hidden faces or hidden skulls. Many great Renaissance and Baroque artists painted hidden faces, including Tobias Stimmer, Leonardo da Vinci, Albrecht Dürer, Giuseppe Arcimboldo, Hans Holbein the Younger, Matthaus Merian the Elder and Marcus Gheeraerts the Elder. Surrealist painters revived the technique of hidden faces in the first part of the 20th century, especially Max Ernst, René Magritte and Salvador Dalí.

Hidden-figure images have also been employed for advertising purposes. Cards depicting traditional scenes of everyday life, historical facts, legends or visual riddles were popular in the latter half of the 1800s and in the early 1900s, and were occasionally given as a premium gift. The object of these puzzling cards was often to find a hidden image – or several hidden images – within a picture. At that time, children were delighted when they found the 'latent image' hidden in the 'manifest image'. This process is related to the concept of the 'lost object' used in Freudian psychoanalysis. Finding the object "is just a process of retrieving something that is already there", Sigmund Freud maintained.

Hidden figure puzzles have long been appreciated worldwide by puzzle enthusiasts. The principle remains the same – a hidden-figure puzzle is mostly a single image accompanied by a caption below it. The text, one or two lines long, introduces the image and indicates the object to be found in the drawing: an animal, a human being, a geometric shape, or potentially anything. The image then has to be turned in every direction to find the hidden subject. Hidden-figure puzzles are classic optical illusions, playing on the foreground and background relationships of our visual perception.

Multipart and composite figures

Mythological creatures shown with overlapping or interchangeable bodies, heads and limbs were popular staples of Medieval iconography. The overlapping body parts symbolised the transition states or cycles by which inner potential could become the actual sequence of events. The

Source de jeunesse

static elements – generally heads – represented a metaphor for those elements of consistency in change.

Composite figures are generally subjects composed of many other smaller figures, such as a man's face formed from smaller feminine bodies. The subliminal message of such composite figures is sometimes of a sexual nature. But it also symbolises the alienation of the identity – the parts become the whole and the whole is both greater than and different to the sum of its parts.

The oldest known multipart figures are featured on coins made 2,500 years ago from the Island of Lesbos, Greece. Some such coins show the profiles of two animals facing each other – apparently herbivores, such as calves or goats – which together form a third, much more ferocious animal.

The Italian painter Giuseppe Arcimboldo (1527–1593) was extremely famous during his lifetime for his imaginative composite portrait heads represented as an arrangement of trivial objects, particularly fruits, vegetables, flowers and so on.

Illusive 'vanitas'

Paintings with a human skull as the centrepiece are known as 'Vanitas paintings'. Representations of skulls in art are legion of course, from Hans Holbein's distorted death's-head in his painting "The Ambassadors" through to Andy Warhol's paintings of screen-printed skulls in gory black and white and overlaid with different colours. Skulls have their place in optical illusions too, as you will discover in the following pages. They are often hidden or suggested in the whole 'host' image. Reproductions of pictures containing hidden skulls were very much appreciated during the Belle Époque, and continue to be popular more than 100 years after they first appeared in print!

Symbols of power, mortality and immortality – such as beliefs regarding the post-mortem survival of the soul – skulls have been employed in human rituals and art since the dawn of humanity. These range from the ancient animal skulls found in Paleolithic burial sites to the curlicued cattle skulls that haunt Georgia O'Keeffe's canvasses. But skulls are not only a symbol of death, they are also a symbol of the duality of life. They are frequently used in initiation rituals as a symbol of rebirth: the point named 'Da'ath' on the Cabalistic tree of life, the gateway to higher awareness only achievable through the union of the various mental states. In a Freudian sense, the skull with its sarcastic smile symbolises the awareness of someone who has crossed the threshold of the unknown - the deliquescence and the transmutation of our ego into the universal consciousness.

Skulls, then, express the equality of all people in the face of death, and thus help us to recognize our mortal nature and the transcendence of our temporal existence. A perfect example is the scene from Shakespeare's Hamlet, where the Prince of Denmark holds the skull of Yorick, his former servant, bemoaning the aimlessness and temporary nature of worldly matters:

To be or not to be, that is the question; Whether 'tis nobler in the mind to suffer the slings and arrows of outrageous fortune, or to take arms against a sea of troubles, and by opposing, end them. To die, to sleep no more; and by a sleep to say we end the heart-ache and the thousand natural shocks that flesh is heir to — 'tis a consummation devoutly to be wish'd...

Iconography and popular imagery, from the Roman era and onwards, often portrays the skull as 'speaking', delivering to the observer a reflection about his present and future life. The message can be heard as a specific philosophy of life or as a moral monition. Generally, in illusive vanitas, the skull says:
- Memento mori ('remember that you must die');
- Carpe diem ('seize the day' - both quotes mean we should live the present moment to the fullest); or
- Vanitas vanitatum ('vanity of vanities', a reminder of the transitory quality of earthly pleasure).

Ambiguous and reversible figures

Does the mind represent the world accurately and unambiguously? Actually, all input signals to the brain are, to one degree or another, 'ambiguous', that is, allowing two or more interpretations. The capacity to perceive and give different meanings to our environment is part of our human condition.

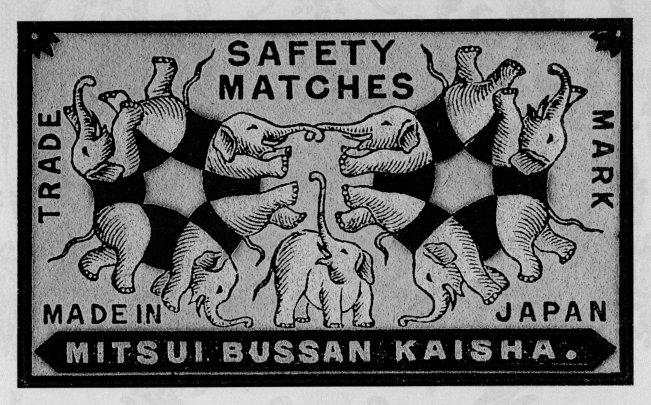

However, the orientation of an image on the eye's retina plays a very important role in the identification of a figure, and especially of human faces. An upside-down world map appears very disturbing (see the image overleaf). Even if the countries are captioned, it is hard to recognize which country is which at first sight, because the offsetting mechanism that should correct and put back the upside-down image in its context is literally 'disoriented'. In effect, faces and maps contain too much detail to work out! Simple geometric shapes can also appear different when turned 45 or 90 degrees – a square becomes a rhombus, and looks larger.

Ambiguous figures are 'two pictures in one' – looked at one way, we see one thing, but looked at in another way, we may see something else. Ambiguous figures include reversible figures, figure-ground illusions and ambigrams. Reversible figures are pictures that can be interpreted differently when rotated 90 or 180 degrees. Figure-ground illusions are illusions that can swap the main figure and the background in your perception. Ambigrams are graphic words or sentences that can be read in more than one way.

Since the earliest times, many artists have played with such visual principles by creating puzzling ambiguous or upside-down pictures. During the late 19th and early 20th centuries, matchbooks frequently featured topsy-turvy optical illusion artworks. When viewed one way, the matchbook would feature one image, but when rotated upside-down, they would show an entirely different image. Reversible figures appear particularly magical to small children. In the following pages you will discover a neat collection of such images.

The concept of reversible figures also interested cartoonists like Gustave Verbeek (1867–1937), the son of a Dutch missionary in Tokyo. He moved to the United States around 1900, where he worked as an illustrator. He is remembered for his series "The Upside Downs of Little Lady Lovekins and Old Man Muffaroo", a weekly six-panel upside-down comic strip in which the first half of the story was illustrated and captioned right-side-up. After reading it, the reader would turn the page upside-down, and the inverted illustrations with additional captions describing the scenes told the second half of the story, giving a total of 12 panels.

(Illustration from Hema Maps Australia, Inc. www.hemamaps.co.au)

CURIOPTICALS

"We live in a fantasy world, a world of illusion. The great task in life is to find reality."
– Iris Murdoch

As conceited as a peacock

Find the vain man in the peacock! This is a vintage illustration from the series American Puzzle Cards.

Question: in your opinion, is the card collection from 1760, 1880 or 1920?

Answer on page 148.

☛ Sailor thoughts

On dry land, sailors typically have just one obsession. Can you guess what the sailor is looking for?

Question: was this illustration featured on an advertisement for Malt Bitters (1923), Magee's Emulsion (1907), or Lyon's Kathairon for the Hair (1907)?

Answer on page 148.

☞ Diabolo!

A Belle Époque postcard with multiple young women that form a giggling devil's face.

Question: was this postcard printed in France (around 1900), in Germany (around 1820), or in Italy (around 1930)?

Answer on page 148.

Pierrot imploring his love to Columbina

A 'vanitas' style postcard with Pierrot and his lover (France, around 1905). Can you see the skull hidden in the picture?

Question: paintings in the 'vanitas' style are meant as:
a) a reminder of the transience of life, the futility of pleasure and the certainty of death;
b) a reminder of the miracle of life, love, beauty and the preciousness of the senses;
c) a reminder of the hazards of life and the possible dangers we can encounter.

Answer on page 148.

☜ Mathematical mind reading

Here is an old DIY mind-reading trick. These four colour cards feature red and black sets of numbers. Ask someone to pick a number from 1 to 80. Then show him/her each card, one at a time, and ask "Is your number on this card, and if so, is it red or black?" After you have shown all four cards, you can work out the number.

Question: How does this trick work?

Answer on page 148.

Are the ribs well formed? ☞

Do the curved lines of the arches behind the pillar meet correctly? This image was taken from an advertising puzzle card inserted in packs of cigarettes (Ogden's Tobacco, England, around 1926).

Question: is this geometric illusion related to:
a) the Poggendorff Illusion;
b) the Lingelbach illusion;
c) the Da Vinci illusion?

Answer on page 148.

☞ My wife and Mother-in-Law

Do you see the profile of a young lady or of an old one? If you observe the picture carefully, you will notice that the mother-in-law's nose is the young wife's chin; her mouth is the wife's necklace, and her eye is the wife's ear! This vintage illusion shows how our visual system tends to group features based upon what we expect to see.

This classic illusion, featured on a vintage German postcard from 1888, was copied and adapted by hundreds of artists and psychologists through the 19th and 20th centuries including the psychologist Edwin Boring, and the cartoonist William Ely Hill who published this bi-stable picture in the magazine *Puck* (1915, fig. a). Another interesting variant of this illusion is the "Husband and father-in-law" by Jack Botwinick (1961, fig. b). There is also a French variant called "Où est sa grand-mère?" (devinette, before 1900, fig. c).

a   b   c

False concentric circles

The 'Fraser spiral illusion' is an optical illusion named after the Scottish physician and psychologist James Fraser, who first described the illusion (along with other twisted-cord illusions) in the British Journal of Psychology in 1908.

The visual distortion is produced by combining regular line patterns (the circles) with misaligned parts (the different-coloured arc segments).

The overlapping coloured arc segments vividly appear to form a spiral, whilst in reality they are just a series of concentric circles. The illusion is also enhanced by the spiral components in the chequered background.

This illusion is related to 'Zöllner's illusion' and the 'café wall illusion', in which a sequence of tilted segments causes the eye to perceive phantom twists and deviations.

Question: the illusion is also known as:
a) the 'false spiral',
b) the 'incredible spiral', or
c) the 'twisted-cord' illusion?

Answer on page 148.

Magic telescope

The telescope shown in the picture is split into two pieces, and between them lies a boulder. Explain why the gentleman can still see the rose placed in front of the lens (hint: the boulder is not transparent! It is a question of reflections.)

Question: is the illustration taken from:
a) the wonderful book *Les récréations scientifiques ou l'enseignement par les jeux* (1880) by Gaston Tissandier;
b) the incredible book *Believe it or not* (1929) by Robert L. Ripley; or
c) the fantastic book *1200 Giochi ed espertienze dilettevoli*, (1929) by Italo Ghersi.

Answer on page 148.

☞ **Whose back it is?**

Is the woman in this Victorian card riding a horse side-saddle?

Question: in the world of optical illusions, is this kind of illusion called:
a) an ambiguous figure,
b) a nasty figure, or
c) an impossible figure?

Answer on page 149.

Woman or skull?

Do you see something menacing hidden in this picture of a nude woman in foetal position? Hint: the pessimistic title of this postcard is 'in the midst of life we are in death.' This is a vanity genre reproduction from a postcard by Gutmann & Gutmann, New York, dated 1905.

Answer on page 149.

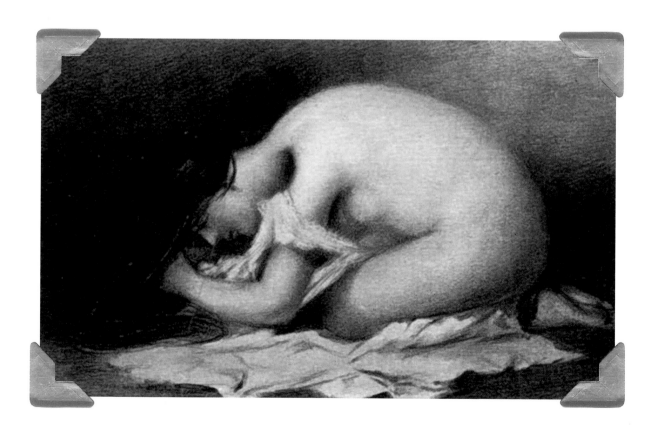

☞ Ouch, the Tower is sharp indeed!

This is a typical funny photograph involving size illusion of the kind that people take when in the presence of historical monuments such as the Tower of Pisa, the Egyptian Pyramids, and the Taj Mahal. The Eiffel Tower in this vintage photo is in the far background, and the man is near the camera holding his arm up over nothing. The camera is just positioned so that these two elements are made to appear as though they were touching. As the image is presented in a 2D plane, the tower seems tiny (or the man seems huge).

Question: who designed the Eiffel Tower?
a) Alberto Eiffelo, Italian sculptor;
b) Alexandre Gustave Eiffel, French architect; or
c) Adriaan van Eeffel, Dutch engineer.

Answer on page 149.

☜ Mephisthophelean face (1)

A devil's face made with nude women, from an E▮▮ish postcard, around 1900. Interlaced feminine figures that form male faces are recurrent optical illusions through all periods. The subliminal message of such composite figures is, of course, of a sexual nature. But it is also a symbol of the alienation of the identity.

Mephisthophelean face (2) ☞

Another example of a menacing multipart face involving feminine figures. In this case, however, the message is not of a sexual nature but implies a veiled criticism against women's vanity. The two mirrored feminine figures on the foreground symbolise the reflection of the ego and are a manifestation of self-importance, or the triumph of appearance over substance.

THE MAGIC EGG PUZZLE.

CUT ON THE LINES AND WITH THE FOUR PIECES PRODUCE EITHER 6 7 8 10 11 OR 12 EGGS

 # Magic egg puzzle

Copy and cut out this vintage puzzle-card featuring 9 eggs, then rearrange the pieces to show 12, 11, 10, 8, 7, or 6 eggs!

Question: This is a card puzzle made by Wemple & Co., U.S.A. in 1880. This kind of puzzle was very popular during the 1900s. Were they known as:
a) disappearing puzzles;
b) vanishing puzzles; or
c) deceiving puzzles?

Answer on page 149.

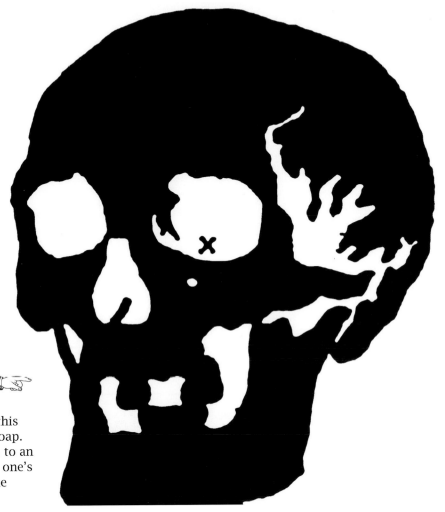

After-image skull illusion ☞

To see a ghostly skull, follow this old advertisement for Pears' Soap. The after-image illusion refers to an image continuing to appear in one's vision after the exposure to the original image has ceased.

Question: the after-image effect is induced by a retinal phenomenon called
a) retroaction of vision;
b) photoreception; or
c) persistence of vision?

Answer on page 150.

Impossible cork escape puzzle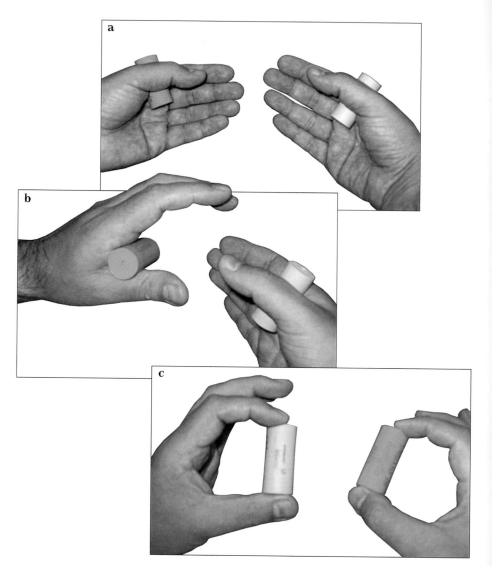

Here is a very old but amazing puzzle that works with two champagne or wine corks! First, drink two bottles of good French or Italian wine and set aside the corks. Then, place each cork into the area between your forefingers and thumbs, as shown in figure a. The challenge is to grab the corks with the thumb and forefinger of the opposite hand – both at the same time, as in fig. b – and remove them without interlinking them (fig. c). This is a great visual puzzle to perform in classrooms!

Answer on page 150.

☞ Is death reversible?

The creator of this allegorical and reversible picture called "Death and the Burgher" was Matthäus Merian der Ältere ('Matthew the Elder', 1593–1650) a notable Swiss engraver. To see a skull, just turn the page upside-down.

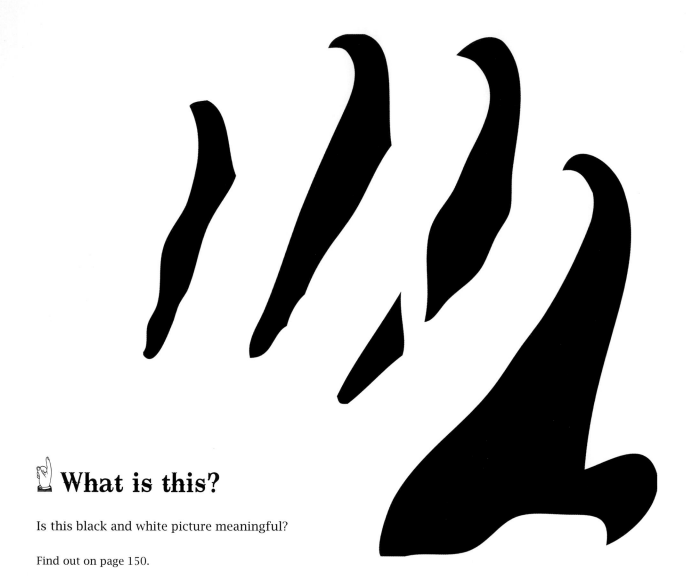

☝ What is this?

Is this black and white picture meaningful?

Find out on page 150.

☞ Victorian love

Another advertisement puzzle from the Malt Bitters card series printed by Hatch & Company, around 1880.

Question: Where is the lover of the reading lady?

Answer on page 150.

🖝 Puzzling lines

An interesting optical illusion involving size confusion taken from the book *La Science Amusante* by Tom Tit (published around 1890). In the scene, you'll see the green lines 'ab' along the corner of the room and 'cd' on the right side of the wardrobe.

Question: which green line is longer: line 'ab' or line 'cd'?

Answer on page 150.

a

True moon size

Two same views of the Luna-Park at Surf Avenue, New York (around 1912). Which postcard shows the actual apparent size of the moon, a or b?

Answer on page 150.

b

☞ Levitating ball

The ball seems to move slightly and to levitate. Scrolling the image horizontally or vertically gives a much stronger effect. This picture was adapted from a design created by Japanese artist Hajime Ouchi published in a book of graphic designs in 1973.

Question: what causes this illusion?
a) unconscious random eye movements,
b) certain perceptual assumptions made by the brain, or
c) slight colour changes

Answer on page 151.

'Vogue' silhouette

Do you see two or three elegant women?

Question: this kind of cognitive figure-ground optical illusion is related to
a) Vogue illusion,
b) Ehrenstein illusion, or
c) Rubin's vase illusion?

Answer and notes on page 151.

☞ Vegetal Holy Roman Emperor

This oil-painting represents the Holy Roman Emperor Rudolf II as Vertumnus, Roman God of the seasons, as painted by Giuseppe Arcimboldo.

Arcimboldo (1527–93) was an Italian artist best known for creating imaginative portrait heads made entirely of such objects as fruits, vegetables, flowers, fish, poultry, books, and... Well, can you guess what else he used to depict faces?

Answer on page 152.

While
you are read-
ing the text within
the circle don't you get
the impression that it is
floating and moving slightly?
Now, move the page toward
and away from you. Do you
notice something special?
Can you explain what
exactly happens?

Mind-blowing
illusion ☞

Follow the instructions written
in the centre of this explosion-
like pattern.

See notes on page 152.

 **Twilight face**

Can you perceive the beauty in this nocturnal ocean panorama lit by the moon?

Answer on page 152.

In the Navy

Common visual troubles in the Navy... In this vintage ambiguous image, the wine barrel seems empty, but it is actually full. Can you describe exactly what is wrong with this picture?

Answer on page 152.

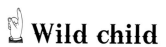 **Wild child**

The famous philosopher, musician and doctor,
Albert Schweitzer, took this photo of a tiger when
he was in Jaipur (1905), but he noticed afterwards
that there was a wild child camouflaged in the
picture. Can you spot him?

Another question: can you tell if this story is true or
false? Answer on page 152.

Visual levitation 👉

'Levitation' is the miraculous raising of a person into the air without any physical assistance (if it's an object floating, that's generally called 'Telekinesis'). Holy men from ancient civilizations all over the world have been reputed to possess the power of becoming light enough to move through the air. Levitation is also a popular conjuring trick, like this one we are pleased to offer to you.

It happens like this. A magician stands at an angle facing away from the spectators. Suddenly, he starts to levitate a few inches above the ground. The effect last for more than five seconds. Finally, the magician's feet return to the ground, and the effect is complete. To perform this trick the magician did not use special equipment or setups (such as wires) at all.

Can you work out how the trick is performed? If you give in, don't worry, all will be explained on page 152.

Abraham Lincoln
March 4, 1861–April 15, 1865

Self-referential president

Observe this portrait from a distance, and you'll find that you have discovered a famous president, Abraham Lincoln! Can you tell why this image is self-referential – that is, a work that refers to itself?

This artwork was created by Scott Blake, an American artist most known for turning barcodes into op'/pop art. With his black and white pixel-like artworks, Blake urges the viewer to consider the limitations of digitized human expression and to appropriate these symbols of commodity. You can see his complete artworks series at: http://www.barcodeart.com

See notes on page 153.

A classical size illusion

Which vertical segment ab or cd is longer? We suspect you already know the answer...

Answer on page 153.

Interlocking puzzle ☞

The giant interlocking puzzle carried by the delivery man is insoluble. You cannot free the three pieces from the puzzle, because it is an impossible structure.

Question: what we generally call an impossible structure is:
a) a structure that cannot exist in three dimensions;
b) an interlaced structure that cannot be untangled; or
c) a structure that is ambiguous?

Answer on page 153.

Pulsating stars

Two illusions in one – the background seems bluish, and the colours inside the star-like elements appear to pulsate slightly. The pulsating effect is mainly due to the high brightness contrasts.

Answer on page 153.

 # Concentric patterns

Wow, what happens to my eyes? This is a geometric visual effect – the circular chevron-like patterns are perfectly concentric. This illusion is related to the Fraser spiral illusion.

Answer on page 153.

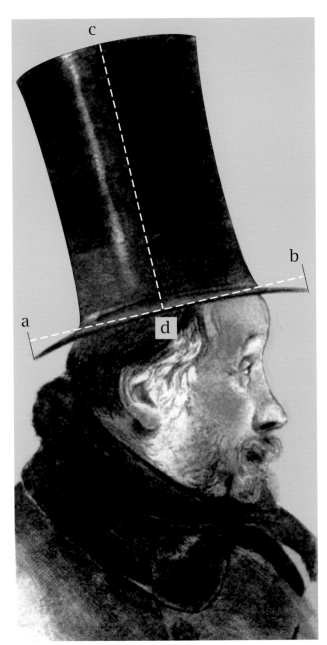

Degas top hat man

In this Belle Époque picture after a drawing by the French artist Edgar Degas (1834–1917) you can see a proud gentleman wearing a particular top hat.

Question: is the top hat wider (ab) than it is tall, or taller (cd) than it is wide? Answer on page 153.

 William Tell illusion

How many arrows do you see? Are you sure? Count them again...

Question: Did the Swiss hero William Tell really exist? Answer on page 153.

a

Love double 👉

A reproduction of an engraving by Cornelius
Reen representing two Cupids (fig. a) with
interchangeable heads and legs (fig. b) called
"Symbole d'un amour inconstant" ('Symbol of a
fickle love'), ca. 1561, Paris, Bibliothèque Nationale.

b

Escheresque endless staircase

If the two men in the picture walk continuously on this staircase construction, what will happen?

Answer on page 154.

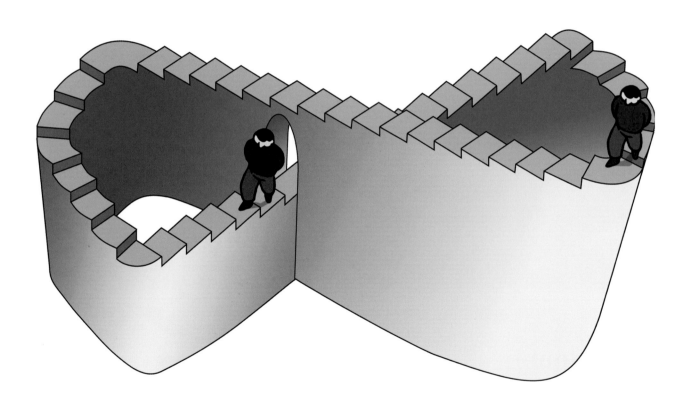

Face in landscape

Can you find the hidden face in this Johann Martin Will engraving from 1780?

Answer on page 154.

How many pairs of horses?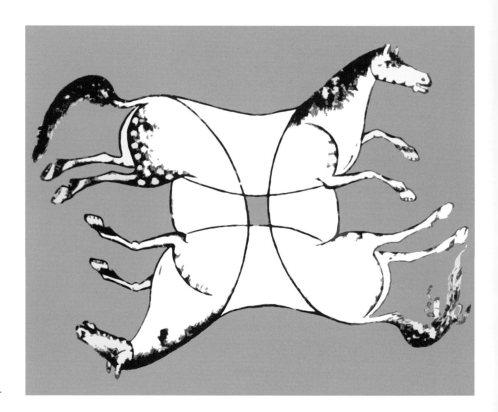

Can you see two galloping horses and two rearing horses simultaneously? This image of horses with interchangeable bodies is a reproduction of a work by an unknown Safavid artist of the 16th century. Safavid art arose in Persia (now Iran) during the dynasty of the same name (1501–1722). While of course nourished by Persian culture, Safavid art was also strongly influenced by Ottoman culture, as well as Chinese and Western cultures.

Question: do you think there is an older variant of the 'two-heads-four-horses' pattern shown in this page?

Answer on page 154.

☞ True feeling

What is the true feeling that inspires this couple? This kind of tricky illusion is called an 'ambigram' Answer page 154.

The worrying literate

Something frightening lurks in this picture by the Hungarian artist István Orosz. Can you spot it?

Question: in your opinion, does this artwork date from:
a) the 18th century;
b) the 21st century; or
c) the 15th century?

Answer on page 154.

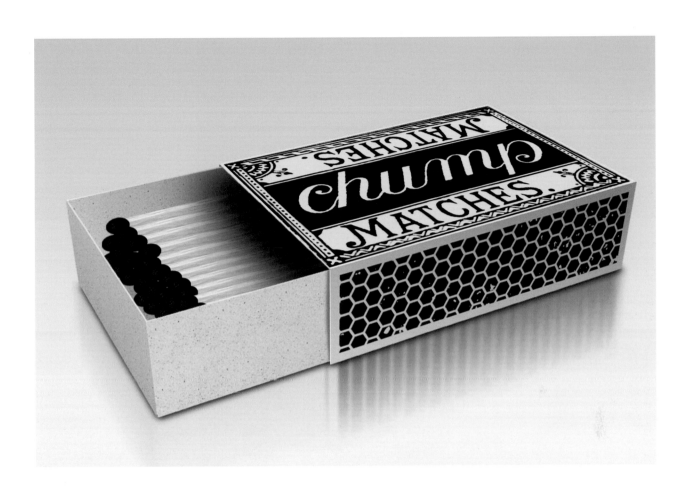

☞ Intriguing matchbox

What is odd about the writing on the matchbox?

Answer on page 154.

☝ The cuckold and the keys of happiness

Life is like a *Commedia Dell'Arte*... In this suggestive picture by Hungarian artist István Orosz, the destination of every human being is hiding. Can you find it?
Answer on page 154.

Two-colour marbles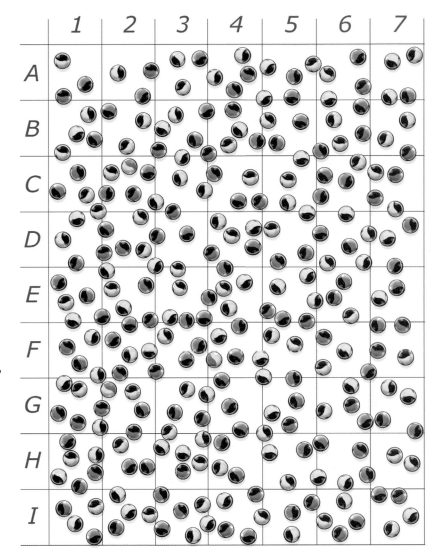

Spot all the yellow-and-blue marbles in the picture: Time allowed 1 minute! This test has been created by psychologists to demonstrate that in visual perception, search is very difficult when you have to find an object with a combination of two identical attributes (colours), than with more disparate attributes (colour and form). This is also a good test of some forms of colour-blindness.

Answer on page 154.

CRÉMIEUX

OÙ SONT LES BUVEURS ?

PARIS. IMP. LESSERTISSEUX PAS. DU CAIRE C?.   DÉPOSÉ

☞ Where are the drinkers?

This is a neat variant of the type of figure-ground illusion called a 'Rubin vase', a cognitive optical illusion developed around 1915 by the Danish psychologist Edgar Rubin. The canonical 'Rubin vase' illusion is a picture with a vase in the centre, and two faces matching its contour. The pedigree of this kind of figure-ground illusion, however, is much older. Original versions of the illusion can be found in late 18th century French prints, in which the portraits not only define a vase, but the profiles themselves differ, each representing a particular person – such as Louis XVI and his family. You now have enough information to find the drinkers around the glass easily! Answer on page 154.

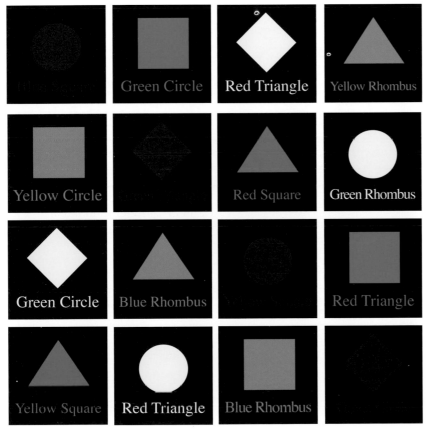

Blue Square	Green Circle	**Red Triangle**	Yellow Rhombus
Yellow Circle	Green Triangle	Red Square	Green Rhombus
Green Circle	Blue Rhombus	Yellow Square	Red Triangle
Yellow Square	**Red Triangle**	Blue Rhombus	

☞ Stroop test

Name the shapes and their related colours in the 4 x 4 aligned boxes as fast as you can. Do not read the words below the shapes! For example, even if the sentence "Blue Square" is printed under a red triangle, you should say "red triangle" instead. Say the colours and shapes as fast as you can. It is not as easy as you might think... If you complete this attention test in less than 16 seconds, you have a very flexible brain!

The Stroop test is one of the most commonly used diagnostic tools when determining an attention problem. It involves focusing on one particular feature of a task, while blocking out other features. The "Stroop Effect" is named after J. Ridley Stroop, who discovered this strange phenomenon in the 1930s.

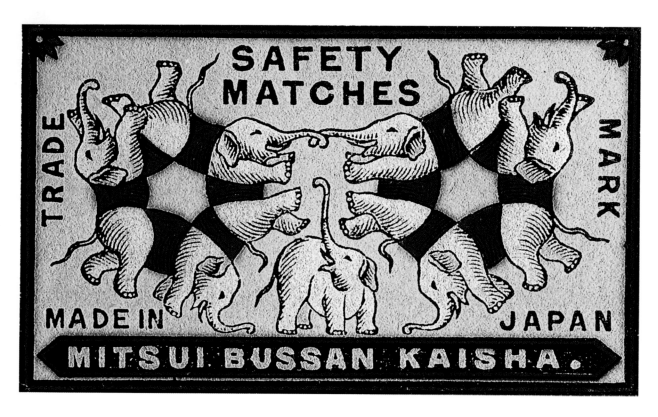

☝ How many elephants?

Here is another example of vintage matchbox art... Can you count how many elephants are in this picture?

Answer on page 155.

☝ Totems

Look at scenes 1, 2 and 3. In which scene are the vertical and horizontal totems of exactly the same length?

This kind of illusion involving an inverted T-shape figure is considered the oldest geometrical illusion, and probably originates from Adolf Eugen Fick, a German physiologist, who described it in his 1851 doctoral thesis *De errore quodam optico asymmetria bulbi effecto* (*The Errors Resulting from Optical Asymmetry*). Strangely enough, astigmatism in Fick's eyes led him to research in ophthalmology. In fact, the first contact lens, which was made of glass, was developed by Fick in 1887 to correct irregular astigmatism. Answer on page 155.

☞ Circus in the clown

Can you find the circus in this vintage artistic representation of a clown face? This drawing was inspired by a topsy-turvy illustration drawn by the artist Larry Kettlekamp ("Tricks of the Eye and Mind", 1974).

Answer on page 155.

A dubbit? ☞

The "Duck or Rabbit" illusion is probably one of the oldest intentionally ambiguous figures devised for psychological tests. This illustration is a good example of what scientists call 'rival-schemata ambiguity', namely that although the image is ambiguous, there is no 'dominant' shape, as both images (duck or rabbit) are equally dominant, depending on your focus or perspective, or simply how you view it. In fact, when focusing one's eyes on the left, the picture seems to be of a duck, but from the right, a rabbit.

Such ambiguous figures illustrate also the role of expectations, world-knowledge, the direction of attention, and conditioning. For example, according to the scientists P. and S. Brugger, children tested with the "Duck or Rabbit" illusion on Easter Sunday are more likely to see the figure as a rabbit, whereas when tested on a Sunday in October, they tend to perceive it as a duck or similar bird.

Thousand of variants of the "Duck or Rabbit" illusion exist. Fig. b shows a neat full-body version created in 1930 by Walter Ehrenstein (1899–1961), a German psychologist.

Question: where did the first "Duck or Rabbit" illusion first appear:
a) in an article by the American psychologist Joseph Jastrow, published in *Popular Science Monthly* (1899, issue no. 54);
b) in *Parapsychology* (an American paranormal magazine, November 19, 1872); or
c) in *Fliegende Blätter* (a German humour magazine, 1892. See fig. a)?

Answer on page 155.

a

b

☞ All is vanity

A neat vintage painting by the American illustrator Charles Allan Gilbert (1873–1929). Reproductions of this illusion continue to be popular more than a century after the drawing first appeared in print. The painting can be seen as either a beautiful girl gazing at her reflection in the large mirror of her dressing table, or as a grinning skull. The lady's two heads make up the eye sockets of the human skull, her vanity items, and an embroidered table cloth form the teeth and jaws.

Question: This style of painting characterised by the presence of an obscured skull is known as:
a) 'skullism';
b) 'vanitas'; or
c) 'impressionism'?

Answer on page 155.

Elephant man

What does this intriguing vintage photo show? A mutant, a rather ugly man or something else?

Answer on page 155.

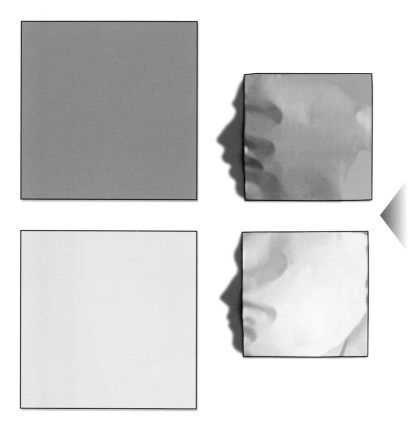

Light direction

☞ Magic shadows

Take two or more square sheets of origami paper and crumple them slightly (as shown in the illustration) so that when they are placed on a wall and lit by a single light source, they each cast a silhouette of a profile.

This admittedly tricky visual challenge is based on an installation by the Japanese artist Kumi Yamashita. Yamashita is a fascinating artist who works mainly on installation pieces that are constructed by using the most intriguing materials to trace figures in the most unlikely ways. In it, Yamashita questions all our expectations, by challenging our perceptions of predictable relationships between solids and their shadows. You can get more info about her art on her site: http://kumiyamashita.com

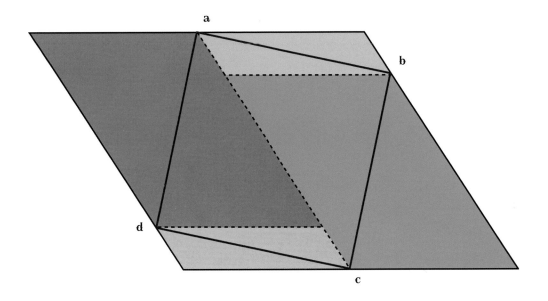

Indecisive four-sided shape

 a) Trapezola

 b) Rectangle

 c) Square

Which geometric shape is more like the four-sided figure abcd – the shape shown in figs. a), b) or c)?

Answer on page 155.

A MAN SHOOTING A RABBIT

 # Where is the hunter?

In this ancient picture puzzle you have to find a man shooting a rabbit. This is an intriguing advertisement label (lithograph) for the toy manufacturer Jacob Shaffer, printed in 1866.

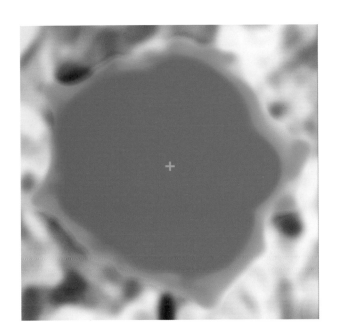

☝ Magenta after-image

Stare at the '+' in the middle of the first picture (on your left) for 20-30 seconds, then quickly look at the '+' within the picture of the rose. What happens?

Answer on page 155.

☝ Puzzled fox

In this 1872 Currier and Ives picture puzzle, entitled 'The Puzzled Fox', there are more animals than you might think at first sight. Try to find the horse, lamb, wild boar, and men's and women's faces. There are eight human and animal faces hidden in the scene. Can you spot them all?

Answer on page 156.

Shàng: high

Red Roddy, Yellow Roddy?

We found this illusion in an old book of Chinese characters. The rods form the Chinese character 'shàng', meaning high. The question is, are the yellow and red rods the same length?

Answer on page 156.

☞ Female ubiquity

Is this woman looking towards you or away from you? Well, you can see her from behind or, if you hide the shaded arm with a pencil as shown in fig. a, you can see her face-on. That demonstrates that the same picture can take on new meaning according to the context in which it is perceived.

Vintage ambiguous cheese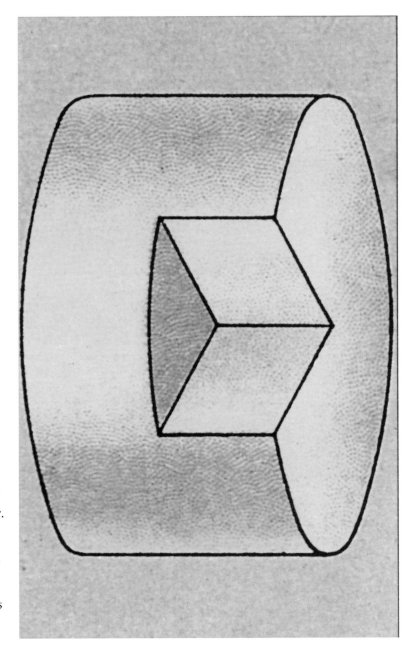

If you tilt the picture 90 degrees clockwise, you will see a piece of cheese under a cheese dish-cover. But if you tilt the picture 90 degrees anticlockwise, you will see a cheese with a piece cut out. This optical illusion was taken from a puzzle card released as a premium gift in cigarette packets in England, 1926 (Major Drapkin and Co.)

☞ Disarmed gladiator

Find the gladiator's sword! This was another Drapkin & Co. gift card for cigarette packets.

Answer on page 156.

T. Elder Hearn, Illusionist

An advertisement for a British illusionist. The scene on stage looks like his face.

☝ The World as a Head of Hair

Published as a postcard, this work by James Montgomery Flagg from 1913 is called "Map of the World." As you can see, a girl's face is hidden in the planetary sphere above. The artist is better known as the poster artist who created the image of a finger-pointing Uncle Sam with the slogan "I Want You! For the US Army."

Walking
Chinese men

Which of the three Chinese men is the tallest? This illustration was inspired by an advert produced by Heinrich Wilhelm Schmidt (Lausanne, Switzerland, 1910) for "Schmidt Teas" and "Wedda, Tea of Ceylon."

Answer on page 156.

Optical illusion improves visibility of highway markers ☞

According to the magazine *Popular Science*, October 1939: **"Optical illusions are now being turned to the cause of highway safety with the recent development by Frank McLaughlin, a Chicago, Ill., industrial designer, of road signs that are said to have a three-dimensional effect, although they are actually stencilled flat on the pavement. Designed according to a mathematical formula that applies to each letter of the alphabet, the sign's property of seeming to stand up away from the street makes it visible to motorists 150 feet farther away than conventional road markers."**

See notes on page 156.

☞ Magnetic eyes

This notable illustration by Aleksandr Rodchenko (1923) was used for the cover of a book of poems by the poet Vladimir Mayakovsky. From whichever point you look at the woman, she always seems to be gazing at you!

Colonial souvenirs

Did the man wearing the colonial-style pith helmet in this vintage 1910 photo really shake the hand of the man with the bow tie?

Answer on page 156.

Look into my eyes, look into my eyes...

This pattern might prove helpful if you need to hypnotise your bank manager into lending you a bit of money! The discs of this notable hypnotic picture seem to expand slightly. The effect is caused by the visual overload of concentric contrasted circles creating saw-tooth visual stimuli. This is a type of 'peripheral drift illusion', or 'anomalous motion illusion.'

How navy's new tricks
concealed ships 👆

According to *Popular Science*, April 1946:

"Based on established and reliable optical laws, the Navy's World War II
camouflage used black and white painted patterns on vessels, producing
startling visual deception that was confounding even at a 50-foot range.
Strongly contrasted stripes in the designs made accurate observation
virtually impossible. False shadows created most deceptive illusions of
shape. Sterns were 'shortened,' gear was 'hidden,' and entire ships were
'heeled' through the scientific use of paint. The ineffective battleship gray
and Dazzle System of camouflage (left) were rendered obsolete."

There is a camouflaged torpedo patrol boat in the picture.

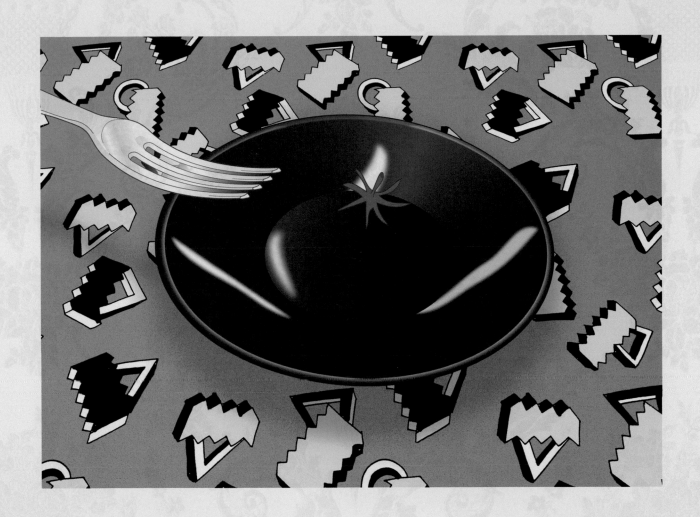

The phantom tomato

Has John really finished eating his tomato? How many prongs has the fork got? Are you sure?

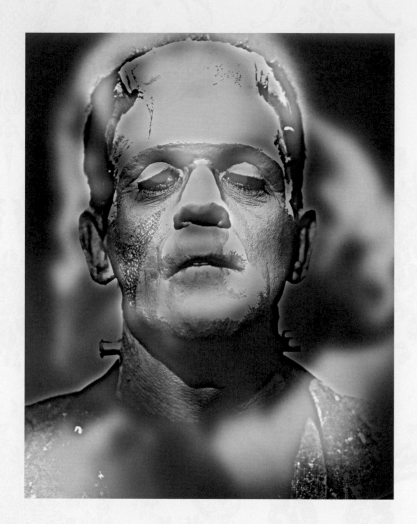

fig.a

Frankenstein's dream

Look at Frankenstein from a certain distance – approximately 2–3 meters (7–8 feet) – and you will see what he is dreaming about. This type of illusion is known as a cryptic or hybrid optical illusion, and is produced by merging two subjects with different resolutions. The result is that one subject is hidden or suggested in the 'host' image. But how does it work?

Answer on page 156.

Whoever makes a DESIGN, without the Knowledge of PERSPECTIVE will be liable to such Absurdities as are shown in this Frontispiece.

🖎 Hogarth's perspectives

One of the first artists to deliberately misuse perspective to create an absurd and impossible landscape, William Hogarth (1697-1764) created a famous illusionary artwork called "Perspective Absurdities," the frontispiece to J. J. Kirby's book *Dr Brook Taylor's Method of Perspective Made Easy in both Theory and Practice* (1754). This work was intended to teach people how to draw in perspective, as the caption asserted: "whoever makes a design without the knowledge of perspective will be liable to such absurdities as are shown in this frontispiece." In the engraving, we note a whole swathe of absurd situations or impossibilities - 20, in fact. Can you spot at least four of them?

Answer on page 156.

👉 The Annunciation of Maria

Here is another example of misleading architecture. This suggestive fresco (wall painting) from the 15th Century was discovered in the Grote Kerk (main church) of Breda in the Netherlands at the beginning of the 20th century and represents the Annunciation of Maria. The painting was hidden beneath a white chalked wall, and was subsequently restored.
A cheesecloth was used to cover and remove the painting which was shipped, after being packed very carefully into a wooden box, to Amsterdam for restoration.

As for the illustration of Madonna and Child from the 'Pericopes of Henry II' – one of the oldest known illusions – the three pillars that hold the arcs should be on the same plane.

Piranesi's prison

"Imaginary Prisons" ('Carceri d'invenzione') is a series of 16 prints painted by Giambattista Piranesi, the Italian artist (1720–78). These show atmospheric prisons, enormous subterranean vaults with sweeping staircases, towering arches and mighty machines. This is plate XIV, "L'Arco Gotico" (The Gothic Arch). You can find 14 sketches of the plates in hi-res, digitized by Leyden university at:
http://www.let.leidenuniv.nl/Dutch/Renaissance/Facsimiles/PiranesiCarceri1750

Something with this Piranesi picture is wrong, however. What is it? Find out on page 157.

First ambiguous figures

These coins are over 2,500 years old, from the Island of Lesbos in Greece. They feature one of the first optical illusions intentionally created by mankind, that we know about anyway – in some of the coins, the profiles of two animals facing each other, apparently herbivores such as calves or goats, blend to form a third, more terrifying animal, maybe a wolf.

Ambiguous and impossible 3D geometric structure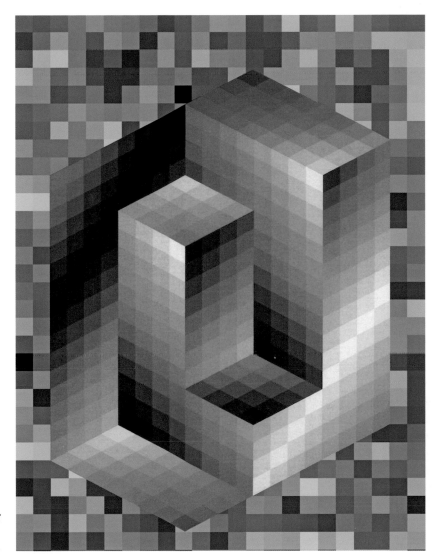

This picture is a study of an acrylic geometric abstract painting by Victor Vasarely (1906-97). Vasarely was a Hungarian French artist often acclaimed as the father of Op'art. This is a genre of visual art, also known as optical art, that makes a large use of optical illusions. Working as a graphic artist in the 1930s, Vasarely created what can be considered as the first Op'art piece: 'Zebra', consisting of curving black and white stripes that are not contained by contour lines. The object in the painting represents an impossible volume.

Dalí's puppies

The surrealist painter Salvador Dalí made this photomontage (1932) starting from a winter sports postcard depicting skiers in a slalom event. With a few pen strokes around the skiers, he succeeded in making an ambiguous image: puppies/ skiers. Before mailing boring postcards to your friends, try to modify them with just a pinch of fantasy!

☝ Pulsating pattern

While staring at this image, the pattern not only seems to pulsate, but you may also see a range of dark spots alternately appearing and disappearing within the yellow disc. Furthermore, the yellow disc seems to float slightly. The illusion is mainly due to the unconscious and rapid movement of the eyes (saccades) between fixation points, and to the bad integration of motion signals in our brain.

☞ Please, can you help me...

Can you help the boy arrange the colour construction blocks in the cardboard box?

Answer on page 157.

Naughty,
naughty boys...

Our grandfathers were great
teases just like us, and
appreciated 'subtle' naughty
allusions and jokes! This
drawing, from a German
postcard (circa 1900), plays on
the ambiguity of the bald-headed
gentlemen also appearing to
be the lady's generous chest.
Postcards with optical illusions
such as this were printed in their
millions in the early part of the
last century.

☝ From above
or from below

An impossible cubic structure.

☝ Magic Xmas balls

These Christmas decorations seem to expand slightly.
Illusory motion of this kind is related to 'peripheral drift illusion'
(PDI) – also called 'anomalous motion' illusion – and is generated
by repeated contrasted patterns in the visual periphery. In fact,
most observers see the illusion easily when reading text with the
illusion in the periphery. Scientists think the illusion is due to time
differences in luminance processing producing a signal that may
trick the motion system.

☞ Just vegetables?

This is a portrait with vegetables, but where is the greengrocer?

The Italian artist Giuseppe Arcimboldo painted this visual pun, which can be turned upside-down, in 1590. Arcimboldo (1527–93) was extremely famous during his lifetime for his imaginative portrait heads, which were represented like an arrangement of trivial objects such as fruits, vegetables, flowers and so on. He was soon forgotten after his death, however. We only have a very few of his originals left, and interest in his work didn't revive until the end of the 19th century!

☞ Is this sculpture possible?

This is an Impossible Triangle sculpture (a 'tribar')
that you can find in the camping site Rosental Roz
in Gotschuchen, Austria. You can check out photos
on their site at:
http://www.roz.at/rozweb/Tribar.htm
(it's in German, but this is the right page!)

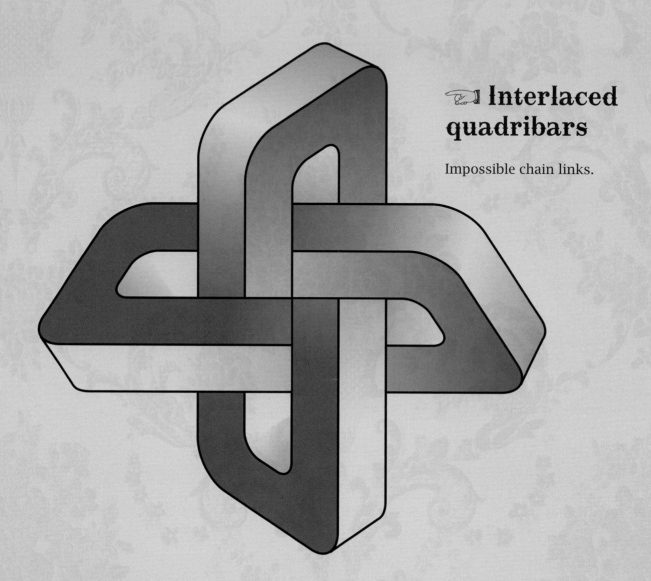

Interlaced quadribars

Impossible chain links.

Vintage stereographic card ☞

Stereoscopy, or 3D imaging, is any technique capable of creating the illusion of depth in an image. The illusion of depth in a photograph is generally created by presenting a slightly different image to each eye, as in this picture, one of the earliest stereographic cards, depicting a tray full of fruits (around 1905).

To see such paired images as 3D, you had to use a device called a 'stereoscope.' You can, however, also see the image in 3D with the help of a small mirror. In figure a there is a pair of images. Try to look at the left-hand image with your left eye, while looking with your right eye at the reflection of the right-hand image through a mirror positioned on the right side of your nose, as shown in the fig. b. You have to adjust the angle of the small mirror in a way that both reflected and flat image merge perfectly into a coherent 3D image.

If we colourize and superimpose the two stereoscopic images, we obtain a familiar-looking 'anaglyph image' (see fig. c), which has the ability to provide a stereoscopic effect when viewed with simple two-colour glasses. In these, each lens has a chromatically opposite colour – usually red and cyan.

a

b

c

☞ The whole is different to the sum of the parts

Can you guess what the parcelled image represents? Only a jumble of dark shapes? Look again and it will suddenly become apparent! According to the Gestalt psychology, we tend to enclose a space by completing a contour and ignoring gaps in the figure, and to organise a stimulus into as good a figure as possible, that is in a symmetrical, simple, and regular composition.

Answer on page 157.

☞ Boulevard Saint-Martin

L.J.M. Daguerre, the inventor of an early photographic process called daguerreotype, took this shot of the boulevard Saint-Martin in 1839. It was lunch hour, but in the photo there is nobody in the street except a standing man. Why?

Answer on page 157.

☞ Spiralling Roman floor-mosaic

This is a reconstruction of the oldest apparent movement pattern. In effect, as you observe the radiating pattern of tiered plumes, your eye may be fooled for a moment into thinking it is rotating slightly. The first attempt to create apparent movement with static images was done by Roman mosaic craftsmen. This floor-mosaic has the head of the Medusa in its centre.

The illusion of perpetual motion 👉

This realistic but paradoxical artwork by the Japanese artist Mitsumasa Anno is titled "The Myth of Sisyphus" in honour of Sisyphus, a Greek mythological figure who was condemned to repeat forever the same meaningless task of pushing a rock up a mountain, only to see it roll down again. This picture is based on the well-known Escher's artwork titled "Waterfall".
You can discover more about the fantastic illusory world of Mitsumasa in the book *The Unique World of Mitsumasa Anno: Selected Works (1968–1977)* by Crowel S. Morse, published by Philomel, NY, 1980.

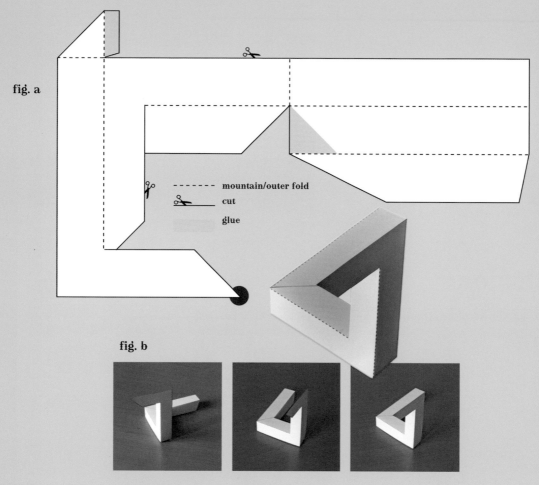

fig. a

- - - - mountain/outer fold
✂— cut
glue

fig. b

Make your own impossible tribar!

Reproduce, cut and assemble the pattern – following the simple instructions in fig. a – to make your own 3D tribar model.

   As you will see, this physical tribar model only works visually from one particular angle that you will have to find with the help of your camera

(fig. b). Depending on the distance your camera is positioned from the physical model of the tribar-to-be, you may adjust the model and try different lengths for the edge marked with the red spot. You may also want to snip its corner angle to get the lines to fit the background of the model exactly.

 # Old barn

Part of this strange dilapidated barn can be seen as something all-together different if you look at this picture in just the right way. Can you find the hidden ambiguity? Hint: you're looking for a vehicle that isn't there!

This is an artwork by the American wildlife artist Rusty Rust. Rusty paints and produces a rich variety of realistic natural and portrait art. His technique and style add up to an obvious love of his subject. He has also produced many puzzle paintings, like this one, involving camouflage themes, hidden objects, and works of exquisite ambiguity.

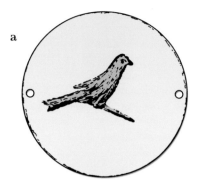

a

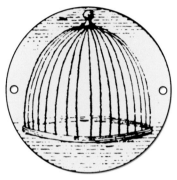

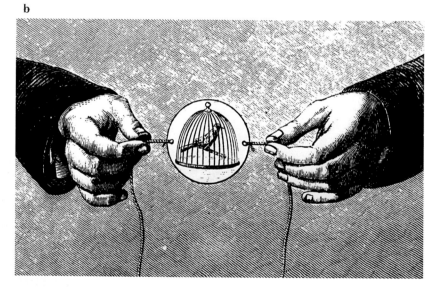 The turning marvel

The thaumatrope (the name means "miracle turner") was a toy that was popular in Victorian times. It was invented in 1825 by Dr. William Henry Fitton. Dr. Fitton got the idea from Sir John Herschel, who observed that humans combine images from both sides of a spinning coin. The thaumatrope consists of a disk with a picture on each side, attached to two pieces of string. When the strings are twirled quickly between the fingers, the two pictures appear to combine into a single image due to persistence of vision. Thaumatropes were the first of many optical toys, simple devices that offered some animated entertainment until the development of modern cinema.

b

✍ What is this?

The white and black areas
form both the figure and the
background... But what does the
picture represent?

Answer on page 157.

☝ The changing wings

Observe the same sitting angel in both photographs. The second photograph is the negative of the first one. Are her wings of the same hue?

Answer on page 158.

Two heads
better than one

An optical illusion in "A Lady's
Orchestra", a comic vignette from
Punch magazine, August 1891.

Spherization

As you move this Op'art picture toward and away from you, you will perceive a dynamic lens effect, where the lines at the centre of the picture seem to dramatically swell and expand.

 # The hidden tiger

"Roar!" This tiger is calling his mate. Yes, there is an extra tiger hidden somewhere in this artwork. It is not easy to find, but once found, is hard to ignore! Hint:

Look at the tiger closely and take the title "literally." Another wildlife painting involving an optical illusion theme by the American artist Rusty Rust.

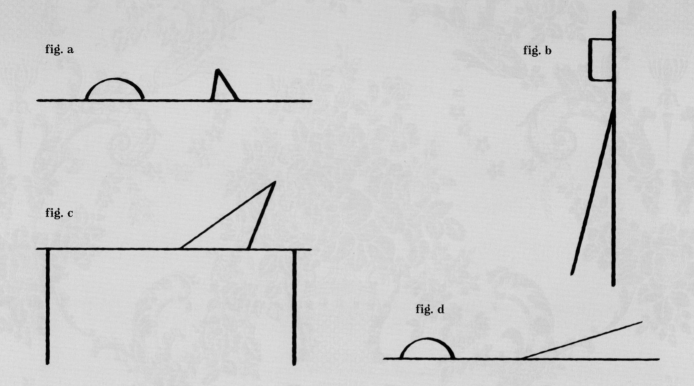

fig. a

fig. b

fig. c

fig. d

☝ Antique droodles

What do these enigmatic drawings by the Italian painter Agostino Carracci (1557–1602) represent? Answers on page 158.

Lingelbach grid

Blue dots seem to suddenly form and vanish at the crossings of the yellow horizontal and vertical lines. More bluish dots seem to appear as the eye is scanned across the diagram. Strangely, the shimmering effect seems to lessen, but not vanish, when the head is tilted at a 45-degree angle. Furthermore, the effect seems to exist only at intermediate distances. Although this has not yet been fully explained, some scientists think the illusory effect is mainly due to lateral inhibition of our visual system.

The illusion is also known as the scintillating grid, and was discovered in 1994 by Elke Lingelbach, the wife of a German mathematics professor.

Question: This illusion is an enhancement of the
a) 'Carpaccio grating' illusion,
b) 'Hermann grid' illusion, or
c) 'Van Heel network' illusion?

Answer on page 158.

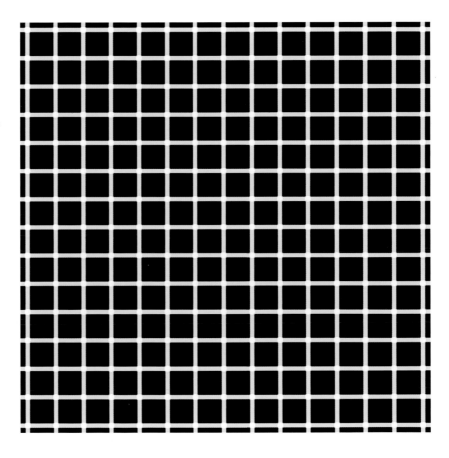

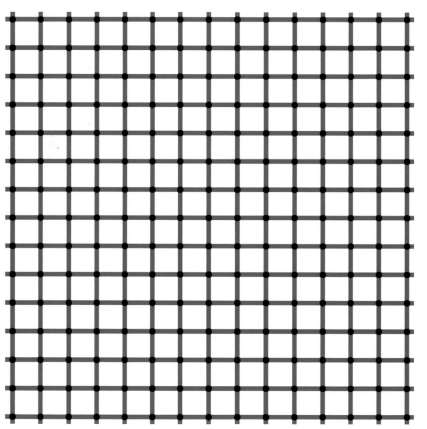

Negative Lingelbach grid

This is a neat variant of the Lingelbach grid that demonstrates that the neighbouring colour of the orthogonal lines influences the colour of the scintillation effect. In fact, you may perceive white flashes at the intersections of the lines in this image.

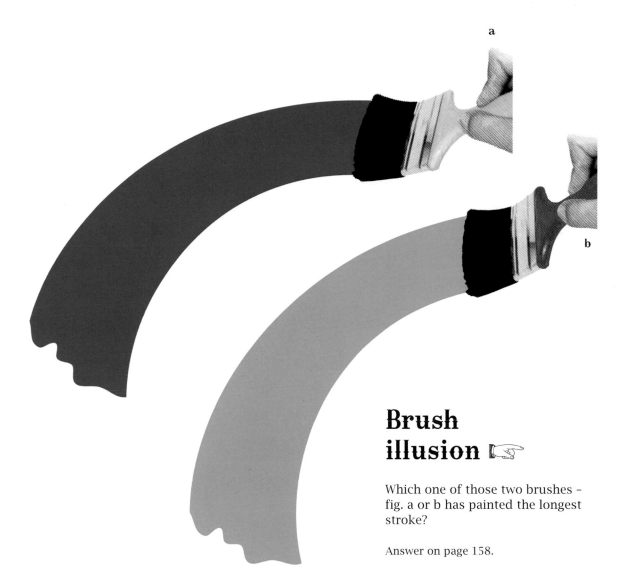

Brush illusion ☞

Which one of those two brushes – fig. a or b has painted the longest stroke?

Answer on page 158.

☞ Hidden panda cub

Can you help the mother panda
to find her cub?

Answer on page 158.

Ambivalent chair 👉

Are you looking at this chair from behind or from the front? Are you sure?

Notes on page 158.

Flashing hypnotic texture

Shift your gaze around the picture... You will see flashing smudges within the hexagons.

☝ Leaning domes

Are these two shots of the Dome of Florence taken from the same angle?

Answer on page 159.

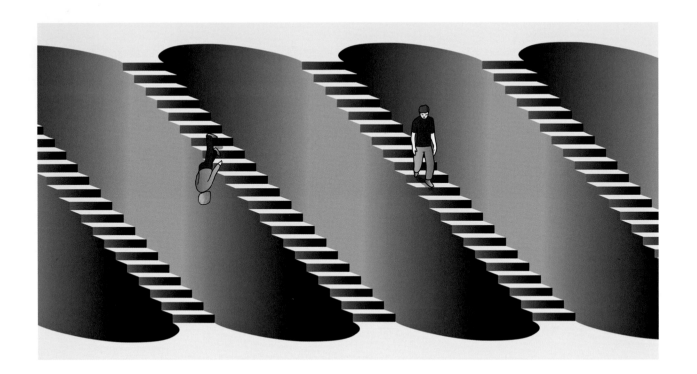

 Reversible staircases

Are you seeing the stairs from below or above? Try turning the image upside-down! This is a variant of the classic illusion of perspective reversal, first drawn by Schröder in 1858. This illusion is also referred as Schouten's staircase.

👉 Impossible building

This shows a probable thing that may occur when you live in an improbable building. It is drawn by the author, Gianni Sarcone.

☞ **Body fusion**

Is the bearded man's sweater white, or is he semi-transparent?

Answer on page 159.

 # My ambiguous rust-bucket

Could you drive such an ancient car? What is wrong with it?
Answer on page 159.

Source de Jeunesse

A Belle Époque advertisement for a restorative drink. It suggests that with the help of this product, an aged woman could appear as attractive as the ladies that make up the face.

 # Hidden world

Hidden in this vintage American advertising card
(from around 1880) are 75 objects including a
queen, a farmer, a lady, a traveller, an innkeeper, a
small child, a boy, a baby, a gorilla, a monkey, two
donkeys, an elephant, a bear, a deer, two rabbits,
two squirrels, three frogs, five dogs, two turtles,
ten faces, twenty-nine letters of the alphabet, a
bird, a rat, two fishes, one owl...

Lost spirit

Where is Lord Byron? This is an intriguing English popular engraving, from around 1830.

Death to our industries!

"What do you see in the Cleveland-Wilson conspiracy?" From the front page of *Judge* journal, May 19th 1894. It is a propaganda piece against the law on custom tariffs. A skull is hidden in the scene.

Four faces!

This is a grotesque topsy-turvy portrait taken from a Japanese woodblock engraving dated around 1830. You can see one face or two opposing faces facing each other. To find the fourth face, you just have to turn the image upside-down.

Concentric circles?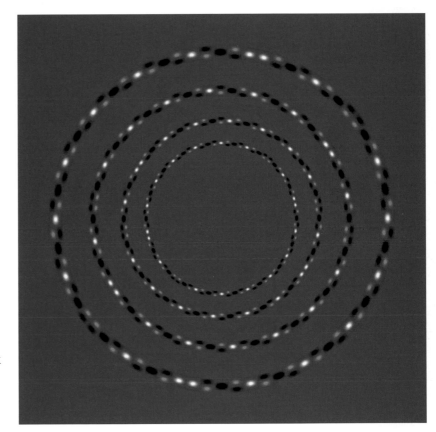

Are the circular patterns of black and white dots perfectly round and concentric?

Answer on page 159.

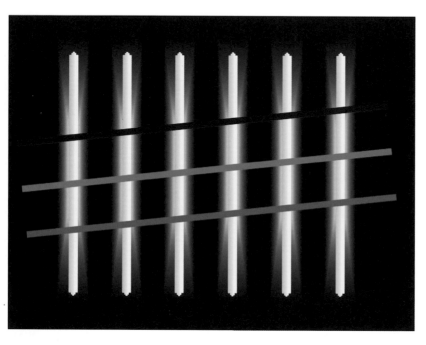

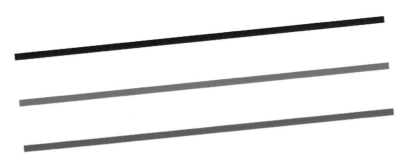

☞ Colour contrast

The three colour stripes in this image appear dramatically different when crossing the neon tubes. Actually, the intermittent dark smudges on the stripes do not exist. This illusion is caused by a visual mechanism called 'lateral inhibition', that enhances the contrast of the outline of an object.

Colour
assimilation

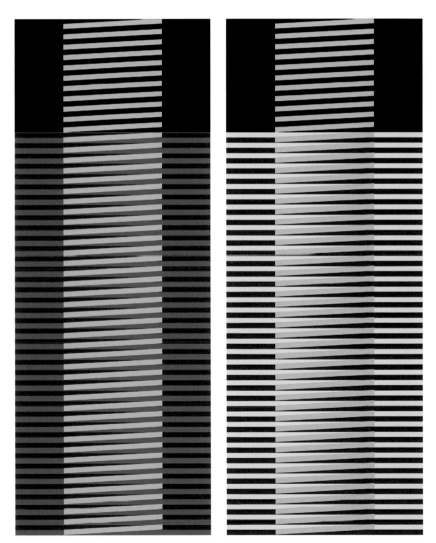

The alignment of the grey bars allows us to discover the effect of 'colour assimilation' – in the first example, the grey bars in contact with blue acquire a similar tone. The same holds true for the sections that touch the red colour, giving the impression of colour gradation. However, the grey is always grey! Colour assimilation occurs when the areas of colour in a pattern subtend very small angles to the observer, making the colour inside the small patterns appear to become more like their neighbouring colours.

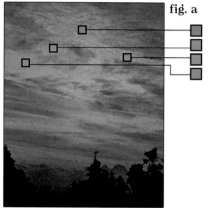

fig. a

👉 Sunset illusion

The painting above contains no blue or cyan at all. The spotlighted bluish areas of the sky are in fact greys and very dull reds. Can you explain this visual phenomenon?

Answer on page 159.

The Arnolfini Portrait

This is a painting in oils on an oak panel, executed by the Early Dutch painter Jan van Eyck (Jan "of the Oak tree"). Amongst other titles, it is known as "The Betrothal of Arnolfini," "The Arnolfini Wedding," "The Arnolfini Double Portrait" and the "Portrait of Giovanni Arnolfini and his Wife."

This painting is believed to be a portrait of Giovanni di Nicolao Arnolfini, his bride Giovanna Cenami, and the artist himself, in a room which is presumably in their home in the Flemish city of Bruges.

Question: Where is Jan van Eyck hidden? Answer on page 159.

ANSWERS

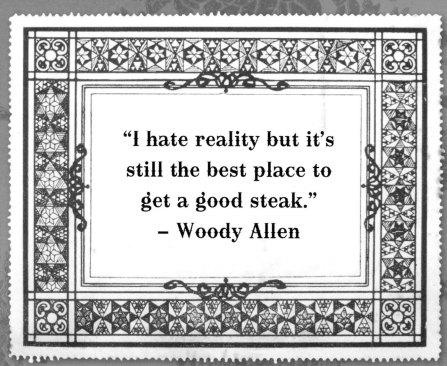

"I hate reality but it's still the best place to get a good steak."
– Woody Allen

As conceited as a peacock
To see the vain man just turn the book upside-down! This card series was from 1880. Another example of American Puzzle Card art is shown below.

AMERICAN PUZZLE CARDS.
Copyright 1880.

THE DOCTOR AND HIS PATIENTS. (Over.)

Sailor thoughts
To see the profile of a nice girl just turn the book upside-down! The illustration is taken from a card series from 1923, known as the "Malt Bitters Puzzles."

Diabolo!
The Belle Époque ("Beautiful Era") was a period in European history that began during the late 19th century and lasted until World War I. So, the right answer was France around 1900.

Pierrot imploring his love to Columbina
a) Paintings executed in the 'vanitas' style are meant as a reminder of the transience of life, the futility of pleasure, and the certainty of death.

Mathematical mind reading
Did you notice that the first black and red numbers listed on each card only appear on one single card? So 1 and 2 only appear on the purple card; 3 and 6, on the blue card; 9 and 18, on the yellow card; and, finally, 27 and 54, on the grey card. These are the key numbers. All the other remaining numbers are combinations of two or more key numbers. The appropriate combinations are indicated by the colour of the number on each card. For instance, number 42 is RED on the blue card (whose first red number is 6), BLACK on the yellow card (whose first black number is 9) and RED again on the grey card (whose first red number is 27). Adding up 6 + 9 + 27 we magically obtain the number 42! Similar magic games using powers of 2 as key numbers were familiar in the past.

Are the ribs well formed?
Yes, the curved lines meet perfectly. The illusion is caused by the pillar. This illusion is related to the Poggendorff Illusion, an optical illusion that involves the brain's perception of the interaction between diagonal lines and horizontal and vertical edges. It is named after the German physicist J. A. Poggendorff, who discovered the effect.

False concentric circles
The illusion is also known as a) the 'false spiral' and c) the 'twisted-cord' illusion.

Magic telescope
The trick lies in the four mirrors concealed inside the telescope's prop and in the table, as you can see from the image on the next page.
The illustration was taken from the book *Les récréations scientifiques*, by Gaston Tissandier. Tissandier was a French chemist, meteorologist, aviator, editor and adventurer, and managed to escape the siege of Paris by balloon in September 1870! He founded and edited the scientific magazine *La Nature* and wrote several scientific books for both adults and children as well. You can see the complete collection of *La Nature* from 1873-1905

online at this web address:
http://cnum.cnam.fr/fSER/4KY28.html
It was digitized by the 'Conservatoire National des Arts et
Métiers', Paris.

Whose back it is?
a) Ambiguous figure.

Woman or skull?
If you look at the picture from a distance, you will see a
sniggering skull.

Ouch, the Tower is sharp indeed!
Alexandre Gustave Eiffel (1832-1923) was a French
architect and a specialist in metallic structures. He is
famous for designing the Eiffel Tower, built for the 1889
Universal Exposition in Paris, France. He also engineered
the internal structure of the Statue of Liberty in New
York Harbour, sculpted by the French sculptor Frédéric
Auguste Bartholdi.
Here is a funny anecdote concerning the Eiffel Tower:
the writer Guy de Maupassant – who claimed to hate the
Tower – typically ate his lunch in the Tower's restaurant
every day. When asked why, he answered that it was the
only place in Paris where one could not see the infamous
metallic structure!

Magic egg puzzle
b) Vanishing puzzles. Figurative vanishing puzzles
involve rearranging parts of an image with a series
of elements (people, animals, etc) so that, once the
rearrangement is completed, an element of the scene
disappears (or reappears).

Because of their visual impact, vanish puzzles are really
striking, but their mechanism is quite simple – the figure
or surface which disappears is simply redistributed
differently on the remaining parts of the puzzle,
confirming Lavoisier's law which says "In nature, nothing
is created, nothing is lost, all is transformed." The magic
is only based on the visual notion that the puzzle is really
different after manipulation.

a

b

After-image skull illusion

c) Persistence of vision. Persistence of vision is the delay time during which the retina captures and holds an image (one-tenth of a second!) before processing the next image. The Greek astronomer Ptolemy discovered this principle back in 130 A.D.

Impossible cork escape puzzle

Generally, most people who do not know how the puzzle is done link the corks like a chain link (fig. 1). Get in the starting position and take note of the bottom ends of the corks, then twist your hands (fig. 2a) so the thumbs both touch the bottom of the opposite cork at the same time (fig. 2b). That is: put your right thumb on the bottom of the left hand's cork, and your left thumb on the bottom of the right hand's cork. OK? Finally, wrap your forefingers around to the top of each respective corks (fig. 2c) and pull them apart (fig. 2d).

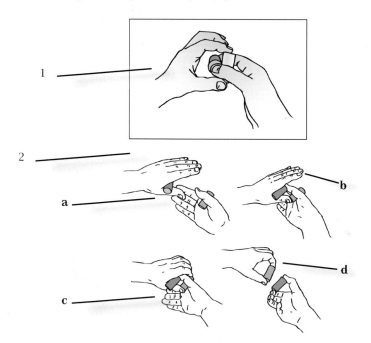

When torturing others with this little wonder, demonstrate the wrong way first a couple of times, showing how they lock together, before taking the corks apart. The spectators will say "do that again!" to which you kindly reply "no." Hand them the corks, sit back, and enjoy the show!

What is this?

It is just the shadow of a person's left hand. Western people are not used to imagining blank or empty spaces as figures. We always tend to give meaning to black, solid figures, ignoring the white, blank interspaces that surround them. In Zen culture, there is a term 'mu' ('wu' in Chinese) that refers to empty spaces as visible objects. In fact, Asians can more easily perceive the nothingness that 'encloses' solid objects than Caucasians can.

Victorian love

Turn the page upside-down and you will discover a man's profile between the lady and the tree.

Puzzling lines

Line 'ab' looks longer, but both are the same length! This illusion is related to Ponzo's and Müller-Lyer illusions.

True moon size

Postcard B. The Moon always seems much smaller in photos than it does when viewed with the naked eye. Many photos you see in magazines featuring both the Moon and a landscape are composite. The landscape will be taken with a normal lens, the moon with telephoto lens, to get a magnified image. The moon in the postcard A is of 'aesthetic' appropriate size, even though it is not the Moon's actual angular size. But what is exactly the apparent size (or angular size) of the Moon? You might be surprised to learn that in fact the moon viewed with the naked eye is as large as a €1c piece (or US dime) seen at a distance of about six feet! Give it a try.

Levitating ball

Actually, the Ouchi illusion is not completely well understood. Some scientists think the illusion is caused by unconscious random eye movements (saccades), which are independent in the horizontal and vertical directions. Since the elongated black and white tiles in the inset (ball) and its surroundings have different orientations, when you move your eyes you induce illusory relative motion at the edges of the ball's outline – that is, between the inset and background regions.

In fact, the neurons stimulated by the circular shape convey the signal that the ball jitters due to the vertical component of the eye movements; while the neurons stimulated by the background pattern convey the signal that movements are caused by the horizontal component. Since the two regions (inset and background) jitter independently in opposite directions, the brain decodes each as corresponding to a separate, independent object.

'Vogue' silhouette

Illusions that generally feature two figures whose contours seamlessly match the contours of another figure – leaving the viewer with a mental choice between two valid interpretations – are related to the Rubin's vase illusion. This was named after the Danish psychologist Edgar Rubin who introduced the illusion in his work 'Synsoplevede Figurer' ("Visual Figures") published around 1915.

You can see a reproduction of the Rubin's vase illusion above, right. Nevertheless, Rubin did NOT discover the Rubin's vase illusion. The four illustrations, right, the oldest of which dates back to 1793, show probably the earliest Rubin's vase-like illusions. You can see, in effect, the profiles of Louis XVI and his family outlined by the contour of various vases and trees.

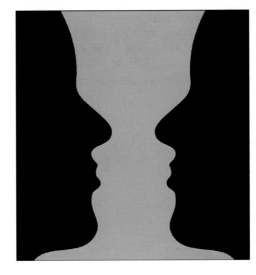

SAULE SYMBOLIQUE,
Qui représente les traits des augustes Victimes
Louis XVI , Marie-Antoinette , le Dauphin
Madame Elizabeth , et le duc d'Enghien.

Vegetal Holy Roman Emperor

Arcimboldo also used naked babies' bodies to form the faces of a lady and her husband in "Eve and the Apple, with Counterpart", painted around 1576.

Mind-blowing illusion

The effects of this are similar to those of an Ouchi illusion, with extra dynamic effect - the blurred drops seem to expand when you move your head toward the image.

Twilight face

The foliage of the bushes and trees outline a feminine face. The image was created by the author, Gianni A. Sarcone.

In the Navy

The sailors will have trouble walking, but not because of excessive alcohol consumption! In fact, the lower parts of the sailors' legs are out of phase with their respective upper parts. The image was created by the author, Gianni A. Sarcone.

Wild child

The profile of the child is facing sideways next to the tigers' eye. It wasn't until the early 1900s that emulsions with adequate sensitivity to green and red light became available for colour photography. But the first colour photographic plate, (Autochrome, invented by the French Lumière brothers), reached the market in 1907. It was based on a 'screen-plate' filter made of dyed dots of potato starch, and was the only colour film on the market until German Agfa introduced the similar Agfacolour in 1932. So, Dr. Schweitzer couldn't have taken this colour photo in 1905!

Visual levitation

This levitation trick is really just an optical illusion. It is generally called 'Balducci levitation' after the American conjuror Ed Balducci (1906-88), who first described it in the July 1974 issue of the *Pallbearer's Review* (Volume 9, Number 9). But the first inventor of the trick remains unknown, lost in time and space. It is an impromptu magic trick that requires no preparation of any kind, just a tiny bit of time and practice, and can be performed anytime, anywhere!

  Like many magic effects, this illusion relies obviously on atmosphere, subtle misdirection and acting on the part of the performer, who emphasises the fact that there are no gimmicks used, and encourages that the area and the performer's clothing be examined.

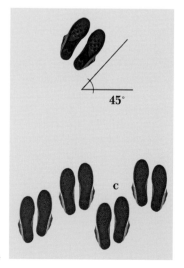

Also, when 'landing', the performer will make a point of hitting the ground hard with the feet, and bending the knees to convince the spectators that his feet were higher in the air than they actually were.

How it works? The trick is to position yourself at an angle – generally 45 degrees – to your audience, who should be a little distance away (see fig. b), so that they can only see the rearward portion of one foot and most of the other foot. The audience group must be small enough that they can be grouped close together.

Then, with the rearward portion of your feet held together, lift the 'near' foot (visible to spectators) off the ground, standing on only the toes of your 'far' foot (the one which is partially concealed) while lifting the rearward part of the 'far' foot and all of the 'near' foot and keeping your ankles together (fig. c). The audience will actually see the heel of your farther foot and the entire other foot raising up (fig. a), which is absolutely enough to create an illusion inside their brains that you really are levitating.

Self-referential president
The portrait of the president is self-referential because it is rendered using 42 small portraits of all the US Presidents. Blake arranged the presidents according to their greyscale density. So, if a president had a full head of dark hair and wore a dark tie, he would paint the dark areas in the mosaic; and if he was balding and wore a white necktie, he would paint the light areas of Lincoln's portrait. The artist offsets the tiles on a beehive grid pattern to produce a hypnotic effect.

A classical size illusion
Segment ab appears longer, though both segments are the same length! The effect of this illusion, related to the Müller-Lyer and Ponzo illusions, is enhanced by the 3D perspective cues of the image: if two objects have exactly the same relative size, we tend to perceive the object that looks farther away as being larger.

Interlocking puzzle
a) An impossible structure can only exist on paper and not in the three-dimensional real world.

Degas top hat man
Even though it seems unbelievable, the brim of the top hat is broader than its crown (ab>cd)! The first known 'top hat' optical illusion was created by German physiologist Adolf Eugen Fick in 1851 to spotlight the tendency to over-estimate vertical distances.

William Tell illusion
In this bi-stable figure-ground illusion it is possible to perceive 8 arrows (see image below). The story of a great hero successfully shooting an apple from his child's head is an archetype present in many ancient West-European myths. The legend of Tell in all likelihood could be based on a Danish saga. The oldest documented Tell figure is a Danish archer named Toko whose deeds appear for the first time in the *Gesta Danorum* (*Saga of the Danes*), a 12th-century manuscript compiled by the Danish monk Saxo Grammaticus. As with William Tell, Toko was forced (by King Harald Bluetooth, 936–966) to shoot an apple off his son's head as proof of his marksmanship.

Escheresque endless staircase

If they perform a continuous loop on this staircase, the man wearing the red sweater will go upstairs forever and never get any higher, while the man with the blue sweater will go downstairs forever and never get any lower. But this is clearly impossible in a real 3D world!

The two-dimensional drawing achieves this paradox by distorting perspective. This picture, created by Gianni Sarcone, is a variant of an impossible construction called 'Penrose stairs', named after the British mathematician Lionel S. Penrose and his son Roger, who rediscovered this illusion. Although the Penroses were unaware of the fact, it had already been devised that century by the Swedish artist Oscar Reutersvärd – and it is likely that the staircase was first discovered centuries beforehand.

The Penrose staircase illusion saw its first publication in the February, 1958 issue of the *British Journal of Psychology*. The best known example of the illusion appears in the 1960 lithograph 'Ascending and Descending' by Dutch graphic artist Maurits Cornelis Escher, where it is incorporated into a monastery where several monks ascend and descend the endless staircase.

Face in landscape

To perceive the face just turn the image 90 degrees clockwise.

How many pairs of horses?

There is, yes. An earlier documented version of the 'two-heads-four-horses' pattern occurs in the *Peterborough Psalter and Bestiary* (England, around 1300). Reversible figures or mythological creatures with overlapping or interchangeable bodies, heads and limbs were popular in Middle Ages iconography, as described in the introduction.

True feeling

Turning the book clockwise 90 degrees, you can read the word 'love' in English (see image below). This ambigram was created by Gianni Sarcone, the author of this book. Ambigrams involve graphical figures or fonts that allow a word to be read (or even to become a different word) when viewed from another direction.

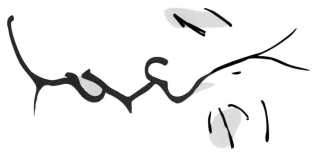

The worrying literate

You can perceive a skull if you look at the picture from a distance. István Orosz is a good friend of the authors and was born in 1951, and so the artwork dates to the 21st century! You can get more information about the work of Orosz at: http://www.utisz.net

Intriguing matchbox

You can read it even if you turn the page upside-down. The 'Chump matchbox' is one of the earliest recorded examples of ambigram design, and was published in *Strand* magazine around the year 1908.

The cuckold and the keys of happiness

Death is the destination of our illusory life; you can perceive a skull in the picture if you look at it from a distance.

Two-colour marbles

There are three yellow-and-blue marbles located in C2, F4, and G2.

Where are the drinkers?

Just turn the page upside-down and you will see the profile of two men's faces. This illusion shows that perception is not solely determined by an image formed on the retina. The spontaneous reversal that you observe involves higher-level cognitive pattern matching, and illustrates the dynamic nature of subtle perceptual processes.

How many elephants?
There are 13 elephants - 12 elephants spread across multiple bodies, and one single one. In Japan, figures with multiple or with composite bodies are part of the artistic tradition.

Totems
Most of you probably chose scene 1, but the correct answer is actually scene 2. Yes, we tend to see the same object as being longer when it is vertical rather than horizontal! The illusion also makes use of the fact that the vertical totem divides the horizontal one into two 'smaller' segments.

Circus in the clown
Just turn the page clockwise 90 degrees and you will discover a clown playing with a balloon, two horses and a ballerina, two elephants, an acrobat on a unicycle, and a dog juggling with a ball.

A dubbit?
This illusion is frequently credited to the American psychologist Joseph Jastrow (1863–1944) who was the first to note this image in an article ('The mind's eye' in *Popular Science Monthly*, 1899, issue no. 54). However, Jastrow's "Duck or Rabbit" illusion version was based on one originally published in *Harper's Weekly* (November 19, 1892). *Harper's Weekly*, in turn, took its image from a cartoon appearing in the October 23 issue of *Fliegende Blätter* (a German humour magazine) in 1892. There's every chance it's much older than that, of course.

All is vanity
Such ambiguous artistic works containing an allegorical theme are called 'vanitas' and served to warn viewers of the ephemeral nature of youthful beauty, as well as the brevity of human life and the inexorability of death.

Elephant man
If you rotate the photo 90 degrees clockwise, you will see a nice little puppy taking a nap! This puzzling scene, dated around 1873-78, was shot by the Brown, Barnes & Bell Photo Agency of Liverpool.

Indecisive four-sided shape
Most people will answer b) rectangle, instead of the correct solution c) square.

Magenta after-image
You should see a colour image of a pink rose. This illusion is due to what scientists call the 'colour after-image' effect. An after-image is a negative 'ghost' of a colour seen after prolonged stimulation of the eye. The odd thing about colour vision is that pink/magenta is not in the spectrum of colours (see image below), meaning it cannot be generated by a single wavelength of light. Our brains decode the colour of magenta/pink as the 'absence' of green.

Puzzled fox

The horse's head is turned toward you, between the trees, to the left of the fox's head. The lamb is seated in the lower left-hand corner of the lithography. Its head is in the tree trunk. The large head of the wild boar is between the horse's legs, coming toward you. The men's and women's profiles are outlined by the trees and leaves.

Currier and Ives made six other such puzzle cards. The most popular were 'Old Swiss Mill', and 'Bewildered Hunter'. Currier and Ives was an American printmaking firm headed by Nathaniel Currier and James Merritt Ives and based in New York City. Currier and Ives described itself as "Publishers of Cheap and Popular Pictures." Their pictures were indeed hugely popular – in fact, from 1835 to 1907, Currier and Ives produced more than a million prints by hand-coloured lithography.

Red Roddy, Yellow Roddy?

No, though they appear to be of the same length, the red rod is much larger (12% larger) than the yellow one. Measure them!

Disarmed gladiator

It is on his left leg's pad.

Walking Chinese men

Curiously enough, the man in the foreground is 15% taller than the one in the background. This is a neat variant of the Ponzo illusion.

Optical illusion improves visibility of highway markers

The road sign would be even more readable if they put the letters the right way up! In fact, you may well read POTS instead of STOP.

Colonial souvenirs

Do you really think that a man wearing a pith helmet would consent to have a man's hand resting on his thigh? The illusion effect of the photo was purely accidental.

Frankenstein's dream

When you see the picture close-up, the fine details dominate (Frankenstein), but when you observe it from a distance, the larger, more blurred tones become more coherent and, in this case, a beautiful diva appears.

A lot of artists used similar optical processes to create ambiguous artworks, such as Salvador Dalí's intriguing painting "Gala Contemplating the Mediterranean Sea Which at Twenty Meters Becomes the Portrait of Abraham Lincoln" (1976).

You can make such amazing cryptic optical illusions too, with Photoshop, by blending together two faces in one hybrid image. You just need to smooth (high-pass) one image, and sharpen (low-pass) the other one. This method can be applied to other kinds of subjects, but face swapping seems especially amazing!

Hogarth's perspectives

The fisherman in the foreground is fishing a line further out than the fisherman on the riverbank. The tiles the foreground fisherman stands on have a vanishing point that converge towards the viewer. The man on the hill seems as big as the woman lighting his pipe from the bedroom window. The flock of sheep in the foreground and the trees on the hill get bigger and bigger as they get further and further away, covering the pub's signboard. The pub's signboard is moored to two buildings, one in front of the other, with beams that show no difference in depth. The church appears to front onto the river, but both its ends are viewable at the same time! Finally, who or what is the hunter in the boat shooting at? And what about the blackbird? It seems disproportionate to the tree on which it is perched... Aside from all these impossibilities of scale, there are also some ten different horizons to the scene, based on the various vanishing points.

Piranesi's prison

In terms of perspective, the arch – which is in the background, emphasized in red   is wrongly aligned with the lower part of the architectural structure, in the foreground, also emphasized in red (see image, right).

Please, can you help me...

No, you can't. The box and the colour blocks cannot exist in a real 3D world... In fact, if you look closely, you can clearly see that they are impossible objects.

The whole is different to the sum of the parts

You may see a knight and his horse in the jumble of dark shapes. Once you have recognized the image for what it is, it is almost impossible for your brain to not see it as that again. The parcelled image itself, as it appears on your retina, has not changed in any way. What has occurred is that while you were staring at the image, your brain was working hard to define and classify it as a recognizable shape. Having done this, your mind stored the new definition of the image for instant recall, making it virtually impossible for your brain to not see it as a knight riding a horse.

Boulevard Saint-Martin

A daguerreotype is a photograph taken by an early photographic process employing an iodine-sensitised silvered plate and mercury vapour. While the daguerreotype was not the first photographic process to be invented, it was the first commercially viable photographic process, and the first to permanently record and fix an image with exposure time compatible with portrait photography.

In this photo, we don't see anybody in the street because of the time exposure of the camera – five minutes! Actually, the street was crowded. The standing man, who had his shoes polished by a shoeshine boy, stood still long enough to impress his image on the sensitised plate, and is surely the first man EVER photographed on Earth!

What is this?

Most people cannot tell what the picture represents. Once told that the mysterious signs are actually birds however, the brain has enough context for the pictures to become meaningful. Nearly everyone knows what flamingos look like – pink birds with long legs and necks, sometimes dipping their beaks into water searching for food!

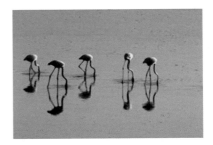

The changing wings

The wings of the sitting angel in the negative plate seem much darker than those in the first shot, but the wings are physically identical in both plates. Artists well know that an object with a standard brightness can be perceived as darker or lighter according to the context or environment in which it is integrated. Such an effect is known as 'brightness simultaneous contrast.' It mainly occurs due to a visual mechanism that enhances the contrast of the outline of an object relative to its background. This is called 'lateral inhibition', because each group of photo-receptors - creating a small receptive field - tends to inhibit the response of the one that surrounds it.

The hidden tiger

The tiger's dark stripes spell out the title of the painting (see picture).

Antique droodles

These kinds of puzzle - resembling minimal abstract drawings whose subject you have to puzzle out - were made popular in the U.S. by Roger Price's 1953 book *Droodles* (the inevitably trademarked name 'droodle' is a portmanteau word suggesting both 'doodle' and 'riddle'). Nevertheless, these 'Indovinelli Grafici' have been known since the Renaissance in Italy. The examples in figs. a to d are reproductions of four of the oldest known droodles drawn by the Italian painter Agostino Carracci.

Fig. a is a bricklayer working behind a low wall with a trowel.

Fig. b represents a blind beggar behind a street corner (we see his stick and begging cup).

Fig. c shows a monk who fell asleep on his pulpit (we just saw his hood).

Fig. d represents a knight riding with a lance on his shoulder behind the fence of a tiltyard.

Lingelbach grid

b) 'Hermann grid' illusion. The Hermann grid illusion is an optical illusion reported by the German physiologist Ludimar Hermann in 1870. The illusion is characterised by 'ghostlike' grey blobs perceived at the crossings of a white grid on a black background.

Brush illusion

Most people consider that the yellow stroke (fig. B) is the longest. This illusion is related to the 'Jastrow illusion', an optical illusion discovered by the American psychologist Joseph Jastrow in 1889, involving two curvilinear shapes. In this illustration, the two curved strokes are identical, although the lower one appears to be larger. This cognitive illusion is mainly due to our prior assumptions regarding perspective.

Hidden panda cub

The silhouette of the panda cub is concealed within the weeds on the right hand side of the mother panda. Even though there are no lines that define the shape of the cub, the flowers and leaves give enough fragmentary information to our brains to make the whole image meaningful. Such figures are called 'illusory figures.' The mental phenomenon in which shapes are perceived to be occluding other shapes even when the shapes themselves are not drawn is called 'Modal completion.'

Ambivalent chair

Face on. But the shadow of the rungs on the seat can easily mislead our sense of the perspective!

Leaning domes

Yes... Both images of the Dome of Florence are identical, though the front of the dome of the first photo seems to lean more, as if photographed from a different angle. This perspective illusion is well known by photographers and is due to the fact that our visual system tends to process the two images as if part of a single scene. Actually, our visual system takes into account a simple basic linear perspective rule: if two adjacent buildings rise at the same angle, their image outlines converge as they recede from view.

Body fusion

Experience teaches us that generally humans are opaque, but sometimes the cues for transparency can be misleading, especially when colours overlap - as illustrated in the picture. In computer vision, an image is analysed, separated into individual objects, and finally recognized. The main method used in processing is 'joint analysis' – that is, the analysis of points where different borders in a scene overlap. Some joints indicate the contour of objects, other indicate interior edges, and some others, colour differences (is the object painted in different colours? or a shadow has fallen over it? or is it seen through a semitransparent material?). X-joints, when two different outlines cross, often represent colour changes for our brain.

My ambiguous rust-bucket

Actually, the car can be see simultaneously from the front, side or back.

Concentric circles?

No, they are not distorted at all! This is a kind of circular 'twisted cord' illusion. This is a visual illusion that is created by images of thin strips of diagonal stripes resembling a twisted cord. It gives the powerful impression that the alignment of the cords or strips are distorted and disordered. The illusion is most likely caused by the responses of orientation-specific neurons in the visual cortex. The Scottish physician and psychologist James Fraser (1863–1936) discovered it accidentally in 1908, after observing wool made from strands of different colours lying on tartan fabric.

Sunset illusion

One reason why the sky looks bluish in appearance in some areas is caused by the 'after-image' effect. The longer you look at the painting, the effect of stronger warm colours (reds and oranges) just strengthens the bluish complementary effect in the more neutral areas. Another force at play is what artists call 'simultaneous contrast.' Both of these effects work together to make the sky look bluish. Of course, we are also conditioned by our life experience that tells us the sky is blue...

So our naked eyes fool us into seeing colours that are not really there and not seeing colours that are really there! The old masters were aware of this and often used it to advantage. In ancient times colours were often very expensive, which is why the artists learned to use a minimal palette of colours to create the effect of more colours than they had access to.

The Arnolfini Portrait

The convex wall-mirror reflects the tiny shape of the painter in the doorway. This is allegedly the first known self-portrait depicted as a painting within a painting!

"The Arnolfini Double Portrait" is said to be a marriage portrait, but also has been seen as a 'memorial portrait', a painting of one dead and one living person, and is considered one of the most original and complex paintings in Western art history. It is actually the oldest recorded famous panel painting to have been executed in oils rather than in tempera.

The illusionism of the painting was remarkable for its time, in part for the rendering of detail, but particularly for the application of several points of perspective and the use of light to evoke space in an interior, producing a convincing depiction of a bedroom, as well of the people who inhabit it. The painting is signed and dated on the wall above the mirror: "Johannes de Eyck fuit hic. 1434" ('Jan van Eyck was here. 1434').

British artist David Hockney put forth a controversial theory in the late 1990s asserting that the natural-looking faces and near-photographic precision paintings done by Jan van Eyck resulted from the secret use of camera-like devices. According to Hockney, some artists of the Renaissance used to point concave mirrors or convex lenses at subjects positioned in sunlight in order to project upside-down images onto canvases that they had placed in darkness. Many art historians remain very sceptical.